IN MY FATHER'S HOUSE

IN MY FATHER'S HOUSE

SEÁN DUNNE

Anna Livia Press
Dublin

First published in 1991 by
Anna Livia Press Ltd
5 Marine Road
Dún Laoghaire
County Dublin

Copyright © Seán Dunne, 1991

ISBN: 1 871311 16 0

All rights reserved. No part of this publication may be reproduced, copied or transmitted in any form or by any means, without the prior permission of the publishers.

Typeset and designed by Michael Dervan
Cover by Bluett
Printed in Ireland by Colour Books Ltd

Acknowledgement is made to the Gallery Press for permission to reproduce lines from a poem by Gerard Smyth from *Orchestra of Silence* (Tara Telephone Publications, 1972), and to Oxford University Press for permission to reproduce some lines from a poem by Derek Mahon (from his book *Night-Crossing*, 1968) and lines by Basil Bunting (from *Briggflatts*, included in *Collected Poems*, 1977).

For my father, Richie Dunne, and Des Gloster

The school was new, like everything around us. Its walls were white and the pillars of sheds in the playground shone with black paint. Wide windows held the reflection of the sky and of the houses across the road in what seemed a perfect imprint. When the windows were open, it looked as if the houses were aslant on clear panes of glass.

I was in the second class to enrol. Most of the school was not built yet and we made our way to the front door past scaffolding where men climbed and hammered. A cement mixer chugged and spun with sludge near the gate. When I stood on the tips of my toes and looked through the narrow pane of glass above the handle on the classroom door, I could see row after row of new desks facing a blank blackboard. In a long and narrow wooden trough at its base, a box of chalk lay near a duster with a wooden handle. The floors shone.

New desks kept a smell of varnished wood for months. They had been made, I heard my father say, in Swift's Furniture Factory near the Back Lane. The seats were so smooth I could slide across them. A white inkwell lay on each desk, set in a round hole next to a curved indentation where I placed a pencil.

The teacher's name was Mrs O'Connor. She was a thin, dark-haired woman with glasses. Each morning, she called out our names in Irish from a large attendance book. The cover of the book was wrapped in brown paper. The other teacher in the school was Mrs Kennedy, an older woman with greying hair. There was also a Christian Brother who was in charge.

The school was down the road from our house. We lived in the centre of a long row of identical houses faced on the other side of the road by a similar row. Each house had a garden. Some gardens had low hedges growing around them, while others, in front of houses into which families had just moved, had nothing and were divided from the footpath by a low concrete kerb. Some gardens were raked and showed traces of a sprouting lawn. Others, like ours, were untended rectangles where grass and weeds grew in clumps.

Our house had three numbers screwed into the wood between a letter-box and a frosted window: 321. I said the address to myself: three, two, one; 321 Saint John's Park, Waterford, Ireland. Saint John's Park had some four hundred houses. Everyone called it John's Park, dropping the mention of a saint as if such a place had no need for saints.

The housing estate was set near the countryside on one side and Saint Otteran's psychiatric hospital on another. There was no through road. The main road into it led from the city centre past streets of small one-storey houses in Poleberry and Ballytruckle. The roads out of it led to the soccer pitch at Kilcohan Park or to the countryside at Killure.

A small cluster of semi-detached houses stood just outside John's Park. They were known as the purchased houses and those who lived in them seemed better-dressed and better-off. They included Nurse Grace, the midwife, and Tom Dunphy, a singer who became famous with the Royal Showband. Like Brendan Bowyer, the band's lead singer, he had once worked with my father in the paper mills outside the city.

One day, a week after I had started school in September 1960, an ambulance passed by as I and some other boys were on the way home at dinner-time. Our houses were so near the school, it was safe to leave us make our own way home. Few cars passed by but an ambulance was a rare sight indeed. It was off-white, a colour similar to the cream that stood near the mouths of milk-bottles. It had a red cross on its side and more crosses on the windows of its back doors. The roof was curved slightly and the engine had a heavy, droning sound.

The ambulance slowed as it turned to take the corner into our street. Then it gathered speed and hurried past the new footpaths. We had a chant for ambulances. *Some-one-is-de-ad; some-one-is-de-ad.* I struck up this chant as loudly as the others. It meant nothing to me, but I liked to say it anyway. We ran up the road shouting it. It was then I saw that the ambulance had stopped outside my house.

My aunt's black bicycle was parked against the wall outside the front door. A brown wicker basket was strapped to its silver handlebars. My Aunt Bessie, my mother's sister, had been in the house a lot lately. She was my godmother and she had a warm, rich smell which I liked. It was the smell of soda bread and clean clothes.

The house had a changed atmosphere. There was a closed, choked feeling about the rooms. They seemed crowded, yet quiet. I could smell cigarette-smoke. Someone placed an arm on my shoulder and I started to cry. Everything darkened as it did when I played in the backyard on sunny afternoons and a grey cloud suddenly blotted out the sun. The rooms bristled. My heavy jumper was hot. The brown leather schoolbag, limp with its small collection of copybooks, lay in the hall.

I was taken into the house next door. The woman there, Mrs Lyons, held my hand and led me into her kitchen. Her children sat at a table, eating while I backed away from the room and stood in the hall where I gripped the handle of the sitting-room door. She whispered and tried to persuade me to go into the kitchen. Eventually, she let me be, sitting on the stairs until she came back with a bowl of warm rice pudding. I cried and refused to eat it and stood at the end of the stairs, holding the banister in case anyone tried to pull me away. When she went away again, I took my hand from the banister and pressed my face against the wallpaper in the hallway. Its texture was heavy and rough.

I had no idea what was going on, but felt as if the earth had shifted. Up to now, everything had been in its proper place. Now, some seismic disturbance had occurred. I was the eldest of four children, but I had no idea where the others had gone to. Four years in a row, my mother had given birth. There were three boys and a girl: myself, Aidan, Breda and Brendan.

Brendan, who was nine months old, had been born on a cold morning in early January. Nurse Grace, who had blonde hair and wore navy-blue clothes, had called to the house and delivered him in my mother's bedroom. I was told that she had taken him from the black leather bag she carried with her. My father came out of the bedroom that morning and stopped beside me where I was playing at the top of the stairs.

'You have a new baby brother,' he said. 'What will we call him?' He held the baby in his arms and leaned over to show me. 'Kevin,' he said. 'That would be a good name. We could call him after Kevin Barry.'

I had no idea who Kevin Barry was. I wasn't even sure what a brother was and was not altogether pleased with this example, the second of the species to usurp what had once been my dominant position in the house. A few days later it was decided to call the baby Brendan, after Saint Brendan the navigator, but for a long time afterwards I thought of him as Kevin, a word that had a different personality to it.

In that same room where Brendan had been born nine months before, and on that same bed where she had lain in childbirth, my mother now lay dead. Mrs Meehan, a neighbour who was a nurse, came and helped to lay out the body. A priest was there as well. My grandmother came in from

Dunmore East. A doctor, who had been in the house the day before, hurried past me and went out the front door.

Neighbours called and stood in the hallway. 'What will happen the four children now?' asked Mrs Jacob. 'How is Richie going to manage?' wondered Mrs Power. My father was a young man trying to hold down a job. He could hardly mind us all, especially the baby. 'You couldn't think of anything worse,' said another.

Years later, I was told how the story of my mother's death had spread through the housing estate. It was talked about on the doorsteps and in the grocery shop, and there was talk of nothing else on the bus to town. There was something disturbing about the way death came suddenly to a place where everything was new and young families were eager to start a fresh life in houses which were mostly less than four years old. Some houses were so new that rubble still lay near gable-ends and some of the streets were not completed.

My mother was thirty-three when she died. In the days after her death, everything became blank. Memories disappeared and became impossible to regain. Only a few memories stayed. One included the pink bars of my cot where I had sat on a wrinkled, plastic sheet that smelled of piss. The cot was in the big bedroom at the back of the house. My parents slept in that room. Near my cot, a brown wardrobe was placed close to the door. A dressing-table stood beside a window. A statue of the Infant of Prague stood on a chest of drawers.

Another memory was centred near a road called the Folly where I sat in a pram with my brother Aidan, and Breda, my sister. My mother was pushing the pram next to a wall that leaned over the road. She was cross. There, the memory ends.

I felt outside her death, as if it was a house I could not enter. What stayed in my mind was the bowl of creamy white rice from which steam rose as I held it on the stairs. A heavy spoon seemed wedged in it.

'Eat it up now,' said Mrs Lyons. 'It'll make you feel better. There's a good boy. Our Mary will get you something to play with.' She took the bowl and spooned some rice to my lips. I kept my mouth shut as I sobbed. The soft rice pressed against my lips. She left the bowl down on the stairs and after a few hours I was taken home and put to bed. I wanted to sleep forever.

The egg stood in a willow-pattern egg-cup on a plate. Its top had been hacked off with the rim of a spoon. A slice of white bread, cut into strips which my father called 'soldiers', lay next to the egg-cup.

'Eat that up now,' said my grandmother, pointing at the egg with a knife.

She was my father's mother from Dunmore East. I looked at the boiled egg. I did not feel hungry. My grandmother stood at the sink, washing cups and plates as she waited for a kettle to boil. She had been to the hairdressers the day before and her neat curls were held in place under a thin hairnet. Earlier that morning, she had gone to mass and her missal lay with a pair of black gloves on a sideboard. A small bottle of Eau de Cologne stood there as well.

'Did you eat any bit of it at all?' she asked me.

'I don't want it,' I whimpered.

'Well if you don't eat it, I'm going to give you away to the gypsies.'

I had no idea who the gypsies were, but they sounded dangerous, to say the least. The thought of them terrified me. Their name had a wild and uncontrollable air.

'The gypsies won't be long making you eat it,' my grandmother continued. She pushed the rind of a rasher from a plate into the fire. It was a big fire of the kind she liked. Whenever she stayed in our house, I liked getting up in the morning because the rooms were so warm. She was always up before everyone else and by the time I got out of bed she had most of her work done. To walk into the kitchen on those mornings made me feel safe. The fire was ablaze, like the fires on a brochure advertising coal.

I put a pinch of salt on the egg and forced myself to eat it: the gypsies were a terrifying threat. The room was nicely heated, but nothing improved the taste of the egg. My grandmother was still an unknown quantity, and I was afraid to push things too far.

'There'll be someone coming to see us in a few minutes, so hurry now and eat up. And don't forget your bread.'

My father had gone to work so I could not enlist his support. My brother, Aidan, sat eating comfortably. Breda, who was two, was away in my Aunt Bessie's house where she spent most of her time since my mother's death. Brendan, the baby, was still asleep upstairs. He now lived with my grandparents in Dunmore East, and when my grandmother came to stay in our house, he came as well.

'You'll probably have to split them all up some way or another,' said someone to my father after the funeral. It was a grim, uncertain time, but he insisted that, whatever else he did, he was going to keep us together. Yet the baby was too young for him to look after. It seemed best that my grandparents would mind Brendan. He lived in the cottage where my father had lived as a boy, looking out over the sea at Dunmore East and facing the Hook Head lighthouse on the Wexford coast. It was a different view to the back gardens and clotheslines that he would have seen from our house.

For the first few weeks, my grandmother stayed in our house whenever she could. My father had decided he was going to keep us out of the Good Shepherd Orphanage at any cost. My aunt would mind my sister occasionally, but we would stay together as much as possible.

The solution was simple: a housekeeper would be hired. An advertisement would be placed in the *Waterford News and Star* and the *Munster Express*. My grandmother would interview the suitable candidates.

Getting a housekeeper was a good idea, but no-one seemed too sure of where the wages would come from. My father was paid poorly for his work as an unskilled labourer in the paper mills. What spare money he had was used to pay for the funeral expenses. Some things were sold off to raise more money. A vacuum cleaner and other items which had been among my parents' wedding-presents suddenly went from the house.

The housekeeper would probably be badly paid and would have her work cut out. She would have to arrive early in the morning before my father went to work, give us breakfast, bring us to school, do the housework, collect us from school, give us dinner and tea, and entertain and stay until my father came home at six in the evening. Every weekday she would have to do all this.

I finished the egg. Nana, as we called my grandmother, praised my efforts and immediately started to tidy away. In no time, the table was cleared and cleaned. It was still too early to go to school, so I was told to go away and play until the visitor came. There had been a number of such visitors and all of them had made me feel uneasy. I was not looking forward to this next one.

There was a knock on the front door. 'Behave yourself now,' said my grandmother. She folded a tea-towel quickly and placed it over the side of the sink. Then she went to answer the door. I left the kitchen and stood in the hall. Through the frosted glass of the hall-door, I could see a large figure. I felt panic rise again.

The door was opened, and I saw a huge woman standing on the doorstep. 'Good morning,' said my grandmother. Her voice changed when she spoke to strangers. It was as if she wanted to make an impression by speaking correctly. 'It's cold enough outside.'

'God, but it is,' said the huge woman. 'I'm perished.' She rubbed her large hands together. Her face was round and red, as if she had been out in bad weather for years. She wore a scarf on her head and I could see creases in the skin under her chin where the scarf was tied. It was a dark blue scarf, the colour of a Milk of Magnesia bottle. Her coat was heavy.

'You might as well take off your coat and have a cup of tea,' my grandmother said.

'Are these the children, then?' asked the woman. 'They're very young all the same, the creatures.' She moved close to my grandmother and whispered: 'It's desperate sad all the same, isn't it?'

'God help us, I hope we can sort something out soon,' said my grandmother, looking at myself and my brother as we watched from under the barometer in the hall.

The two women went back into the kitchen and we went upstairs to our bedroom to play. It was cold there, but we were told to keep out of the way for a while. I could hear their talk and the clatter of their cups. They spoke quietly and I could picture my grandmother's face by the sound of her voice. After what seemed an age, I heard them standing up. Tea-things were lifted and set down. A tap was turned and water poured into a kettle. Biscuits were moved on a plate. The kitchen door opened and they came out.

'Well, what's your name?' the woman said to me.

I held onto my grandmother's coat which was hanging at the end of the stairs. 'I'd say you're Aidan, are you?'

'That's Seán,' my grandmother told her. 'He's not always

that quiet, mind you.'

'You're a fine big man alright,' the woman said. 'I'd say you're a bit of a rascal.'

I was silent. Her face was more red than ever now that she had been in the hot kitchen. Her eyes were watery.

I drew back from her hand when she bent to pat my head. 'He's very shy,' she said. 'He'll grow out of that. It's no wonder with all that's after happening.'

My grandmother said nothing but just looked at me. Her arms were folded and her face wore a worried look. The woman dipped her finger into the holy water fount nailed to the wall, blessed herself and then, after putting on her coat and scarf, said goodbye and left.

My grandmother stood quietly in the hall. We stood looking up at her as if waiting for sweets. She fingered the small gold cross that was hanging from a chain around her neck. Then she snapped out of her daydream and looked at her watch. 'Look at the time,' she said. 'You'll be dead late for school. Quick. Get on your coats. Come on now.' Holding Aidan's hand, I ran down the road. My grandmother stood at the door. We passed the large woman near Roche's Corner at the end of the street and pretended not to notice her. That was the last I ever saw of her.

Tessie Ryan got the job. Tessie lived in a small house in the centre of Waterford. It was in the Back Lane, or Saint John's Lane, as it was properly called. Her father had served as a British soldier in the First World War.

Her brother, Tom, had died when still a boy, and her sister, Bridie, lived in Birmingham. From what I heard, I gathered that her mother had had a hard life rearing her children. Her father went to an office in Barrack Street once a week to collect his British Army pension, and one of her mother's main aims in life was to ensure that the money ended up in the house and not in a pub's till. Her father was a quiet man but when drink took him over he changed into a raging, furious victim of war and poverty. Memories of the war invaded his mind and he stopped to fight and shout on the footpaths of Waterford as if the streets were filled with German soldiers lurching towards trenches.

Many men from Waterford joined the British Army during the Great War. They had been urged to enlist by John Redmond, a Wexfordman who had been MP for New Ross. His name was a potent force for many Waterford people long after his death. The Waterford branch of Fine Gael had a sharp Redmondite tinge to it, and Redmond's name was often invoked with some solemnity in the leader columns of the *Munster Express.*

One day I saw an old man drunk on Ballybricken Hill, where huge political meetings had been held in the past. It had been a prime Redmondite area. The old man tottered along the footpath, falling every few steps, but righting himself just in time against the plate-glass windows of a supermarket. He waved his hand in the air and shouted: 'Up Redmond! Up Redmond!'

In Tessie's mother's prayer-book there were a number of memorial cards and among them was one for Major Willie Redmond, John Redmond's brother. The name of John Redmond had a force in that household that was equalled, I would learn, by the force of de Valera's in my own.

'Any good I ever got, I got from England,' Tessie would say. 'I got feck all from this country.' She wore a poppy on Poppy Day, bought from British Legion supporters on the streets of Waterford, and had worked in England during the

Second World War at a time when many young women left Waterford and other Irish cities to work in English munitions factories. She became ill with a brain haemorrhage and came home, weaker by far and capable only of limited activity.

A few weeks after my mother's death, my father employed Tessie to look after us. My grandmother interviewed her, as she had interviewed all the others, and she met my father. She passed whatever stringent tests my grandmother set, and arrived also with a good word from one of her neighbours in the Back Lane who worked with my father in the paper mills.

My relationship with Tessie was strained from the start. I was never as close to her as Aidan and Breda were to become. My memories of my mother were strong and I clung to them in a frightened and morbid way. When Tessie came from town to meet us for the first time, I hid behind coats hanging in the hall and wanted to have nothing to do with her.

On the younger side of forty, she was blonde-haired and wore glasses, and when she bent down I could see the tops of her nylon stockings joined to the straps of a girdle. She wore false teeth and had a way of making her dentures stick out in front of her mouth like a funny face from a comic. Every morning, she got the bus from town and helped us to get ready for school. She always had a shopping-bag with her. It had the same sort of things in it every day: bunches of soft bananas bought in Bowe's vegetable shop near her house; talcum powder; a black purse full of coins and old bus-tickets; a packet of Player's untipped cigarettes and a box of matches; tins of cat food; knitting; paper bags of boiled sweets. Each of these things had its own smell and they blended in an odour that was unmistakably hers.

She got on especially well with Aidan. He was often ill and out of school and so she came to spend more time with him than with Breda or myself. With Breda, she was strict but just as close. She enlisted her help in the daily routine of housework, sending her to the shop or having her help with the cleaning of floors and the making of beds.

I resisted her to the core. It was not so much that I disliked her but a part of me refused to believe that she was happening. At times, I cut myself off from her and took to reading as a way of escape. At other times, things went smoothly and, as I grew older, she was as involved as a parent in events like the preparations for my first communion or the lead-up to a school concert.

My occasionally obstreperous and stubborn resistance made things difficult for Tessie because, at the best of times, she treated us as if we were the children she otherwise would never have. She was constantly buying us treats and small gifts. When she went over to see her sister in Birmingham, she came back with toys and other presents, like a set of children's knives and forks, to which we looked forward with huge excitement and which gave the very name of England an association with colourful largesse.

The work she put into rearing us and into housekeeping went beyond what she was paid for. She would not have seen it that way. She had a feeling for underdogs, a category into which my father fitted neatly.

Tessie loved to sing. There was a small shop near her home which sold second-hand books, comics and song-sheets. It was called Stickyback Power's. There she bought the words of many songs at a penny a sheet. She gave them to me later, so I acquired a repertoire of songs that were standard favourites long before I was born. Working at the sink or sewing by the fire, she sang these songs herself: 'Beautiful Dreamer'; 'Che Sera Sera'; 'Scarlet Ribbons'; 'Clementine'.

When she talked of her time in England, Tessie often referred to music. Names like Gracie Fields and Vera Lynn became as familiar to me as the Beatles and the Rolling Stones. She spoke of going to theatres in England and of the music-hall, and showed me what a knees-up was, lifting her dress up above her knees and dancing around the kitchen as I stared in excitement and embarrassment at the varicose veins on her white legs and at the large pair of faded pink knickers that ballooned around her waist as she danced late in the afternoon after listening to Mrs. Dale's Diary on the wireless.

She listened mostly to English radio stations. 'I was in London during the war,' she told us. 'The Blitz it was called. And when the German aeroplanes came attacking, the English people would start shouting. "They're dropping bums! The bums are falling!" That's what they'd say.' Breda laughed so much at this that she went red and nearly choked on her dinner. I had seen the word 'bum' in a book by Walter Macken on the sitting-room bookshelf and had laughed then as well.

When summer came, Tessie took us to Tramore on the bus. (As a girl, she had often gone to Tramore, taking the train that now no longer ran. She went with her sister to dancehalls and marquees, on the look-out for a man or just out for music and fun). Tessie trooped us off to the beach where we changed into swimming-togs while she arranged a picnic on the sand.

Before we left home, she stacked slices of bread on the kitchen table and made sandwiches with slices of luncheon sausage, a pale pink meat that was sold cheaply in Jackie O'Regan's shop. Other sandwiches had sliced banana in them. She took a big bottle of lemonade — a Big Brother as she called it — as well. By the time we started to eat, there was usually sand in everything. Bits of it stuck in my teeth as I chewed on a sandwich. The banana sandwiches had gone soft, brown and mushy. Grains of sand flecked the inside of the lemonade bottle. When I wiped my mouth with a towel, there was sand on that as well.

After a swim, Tessie took us to the amusement arcades. She

gave us a fixed number of pennies from the stray coins that had accumulated at the bottom of her bag. She enjoyed gambling, and in summer played the amusement arcades in Tramore and sometimes went to an arcade near her house. In winter, she played bingo or cards. She smoked an endless number of cigarettes and always had a pot of tea to hand — Lyons' tea, weak with lots of milk; my father liked it strong with little. 'I'd be lost without the cup of tea,' she would say. 'We're out of sugar. Feck it. Breda, get a cup out of the press and run in to Mrs Jacob and ask for the loan of a cup of sugar until the messages come on Wednesday.' She lit another cigarette as she waited, and I came to know the face of the bearded sailor on the Player's cigarette packet as well as an old family photograph.

After her mother died, Tessie lived alone in the house in John's Lane. A photograph of her long-dead brother was on one wall. Thoughts of her father and his khaki uniform could make her turn as sentimental as the songs she sang.

There was a small park across the road from her house and it was here, near the playground, that I kissed her niece from Birmingham when I was seven: my first experience of such an event. I had known for ages that she was coming to stay. Tessie teased me about her arrival. 'She's like a filmstar,' she said about the six-year-old Edwina. 'She has long black hair and she's very good in school, the same as you. You'll be a match for each other.' She had us more or less married off by the time the girl arrived with her mother. I kissed her on the cheek simply to see what it was like. I approved of the sensation, though she did not seem very interested. When she went back to England I pined for her, or thought I did.

At the bottom of the park, an old graveyard was sealed off by a wall. Through a gap in a metal door I could see lines of old headstones set against a wall overgrown with ivy. No-one ever went in there and, before going to sleep, I drew the sheets tightly around my face as I imagined those headstones moving and the park teeming with dancing skeletons.

By day, the park held no such terror. Tessie sat knitting and smoking on a bench as we played on the paths or in the grass. The people who sat with her came mostly from the inner-city houses near her own.

One of her friends was an old woman called May Cleary to whose house Tessie would often take us; it was just around the corner from John's Lane. May Cleary always sat in an armchair by the fire, settled in a mass of dark clothes and drawing me towards her as she talked of Ireland's fight for freedom. She showed me a gap in the wall where guns had once been hidden at the time of the Black and Tans. She called me *alanna* and showed me green-covered books about Robert Emmet, Thomas Ashe and other patriots.

'When are you going to join the Legion?' she asked me. She was referring to the Legion of Mary, a charity organisation founded by a Dubliner named Frank Duff. He came to Waterford one evening to give a talk after a slide show about a missionary named Edel Quinn. Tessie took me along to hear him.

Edel Quinn came from Kanturk in County Cork and died at a young age when working for the conversion of pagans in Nigeria. A picture of her simple grave appeared on the screen. Another slide showed her young face. With her suffering, early death and general air of beatification, I enlisted her next to my mother in my roll of morbid martyrdom and prayed to her frequently, getting to the point where I told Tessie she was sending me personal messages. Frank Duff spoke of her with great admiration. He refused most of the food offered to him after the slide show and ate mostly plain bread and jam, with no butter. Tessie took this as a sure sign of holiness.

Annie Maher was another of Tessie's friends. She lived in a

house in John's Street which had been a small shop before Annie became too old to run a business. She was a thin, frail woman with a cracked voice. She always wore a beret and hairs sprouted on her chin. She frequently talked to her brother, Matt, who had been dead for some years, but who seemed nonetheless to answer her questions from a point somewhere on the kitchen wall. Her house had a smell of melted butter.

Tessie visited these women and sat with them for hours. She went shopping for them and was happy in their company during the evenings. She had few friends. Like herself, they lived in the very centre of town but their world was far from the glamour of large shops like Woolworths and Shaws. Instead, it was a place of huddled houses and small, closed-up shops. They used words like 'huckster' to describe a shop and when they spoke of their past they would refer to it as their 'heyday'. In their small, dark houses, the lights were often left on during the day. They were all fond of cats.

Cats followed Tessie around like a loyal congregation. They lay curled in her lap or stalked her kitchen table and stuck their noses in empty cat-food tins. They lay in boxes where they gave birth. They licked themselves clean by the fire. She was always buying tins of cat-food, the smell of which I hated, and she thought nothing of adopting whatever cats were lured from neighbouring backyards and alleyways to her own kitchen. Her own sense of smell had been damaged by the effects of her brain haemorrhage, so she never realised how overpowering the smell of cat-piss and cat-food could be.

She loved to hear me sing and was delighted when, aged ten, I sang in variety concerts in the Town Hall. The word went around that I had a very good soprano voice and concert-organisers would call to the door to ask my father if I could sing in some forthcoming event. My father would come into the kitchen to ask me, but I would always say no. I had seen some film of Mario Lanza's in which he played the part of a cantankerous tenor, so I assumed that great singers were always difficult.

My father would ask me again, aware that an important person was waiting at the door. After a fuss, I would agree. Sister Augustine, from the Ursuline Convent, gave me lessons and I also sang in the church choir. Singing on stage for the first time in the Town Hall marked the peak of my career. Tessie sat holding my coat, the tears running down her face as I sang 'Panis Angelicus', my tongue gliding over the lovely Latin words that I only half-understood. I sang in many concerts and Tessie was always in the audience.

Years after she first came to our house, my voice cracked and broke. I was to sing 'The Holy City' in a concert on the stage of the Town Hall. There are a number of very high notes in the song. Normally, I would take these with ease. I was fine for most of the song but towards the end a strange feeling crept into my throat. It was a slight, harsh quiver. As I edged towards the last high notes, I knew I could never reach them. I stood in the full glare of a spotlight. I could see no more than the first few rows in the audience. My voice went like an escaped butterfly from my mouth and the song ended in a croak. I went home on the bus afterwards knowing I would never sing on that stage again.

With my lost soprano voice, something else died as well. My singing had been a single strong link with Tessie. Now that it was gone, it was as if a frail thread that joined us was breaking and there would be nothing left only the two of us, with less and less in common — myself with my resentment that faded but never died, and Tessie with her old-fashioned songs and her stories about England that failed to make me laugh anymore.

Until that time came, we lived in uneasy harmony. Unlike the fat woman my grandmother had interviewed, Tessie was here to stay. I would have to make the best of it, but somewhere inside there was a hollow space that nothing could fill.

'Go down to the bus stop and meet your Grandad,' said my father one Saturday when I was eight. 'You're big and bold enough now to do it without me.'

Aidan went with me. We held hands as we crossed the road near the school. Grandad sometimes came from Dunmore East on Saturday evening and spent what was left of the weekend with us. He got the bus to Waterford and another from town to John's Park. At the second last stop, across the road from a small shop, he got off and made for our house.

'Oh be the hokey,' he said when the bus was gone. His smell was always the same, a heavy tang of Woodbines and Guinness. As he got off the bus, he swayed slightly and leaned a hand on my shoulder. He felt heavy. I was terrified of slipping and falling on the footpath, bringing him down with me. I was not so much frightened of getting hurt as of looking a fool, lying there on the ground with my grandfather on top of me and his cap down over one eye.

'Hold on a minute there now,' he said. He swayed again like a ship. Then, he steadied himself and placed a bag on the ground. He straightened up, looked around, and leaned forward again. This time he placed one hand on my shoulder and the other on Aidan's. 'By God, but ye're two great men'. His fingertips were stained a heavy brown. He took his hands from our shoulders and bent to pick up his bag, a coarse, striped affair in which I could barely see the glinting caps of a half-dozen bottles.

The bottles clinked when he eventually stirred and walked.

Leaning against walls or hedges, he slowly made his way to our house as we walked along beside him. Near Roche's Corner at the end of our street, he fell heavily against the hedge and, when he hauled himself away, a kind of rough mould was left on the privet.

Once inside the house, my grandfather went to the toilet and then, a new man, made straight for his favourite chair near the fire, settling with the contentment of a cat into a cushion. He wore a white shirt, a red jumper with no sleeves, and a cap always. I wondered if it was stuck to his few hairs underneath.

He worked on the quayside at Dunmore East, and when I went to see him there one day he bent down and pretended to pick a sixpence from the ground. 'I found this in a net,' he said, and pressed it into my palm. Most of his life seemed to have been spent around that harbour. He had worked on boats and for many years had served on the lifeboat as well. On the wall over the door of the parlour in his house, a framed certificate commemorated his lifeboat work.

His father's name was Richard, and the family came from Knockapadden, just a few miles beyond Dunmore East. My grandfather was one of eleven children, with one of whom, a brother, he later had a terrible row over some forgotten cause. They never spoke again. One of his sisters died in childhood and was buried in Rathmoylan churchyard. Someone told me that bones and skulls were scattered throughout that ruined graveyard and I felt nervous whenever I passed it in case the child-like ghost of my grand-aunt might float out of the ditch.

My grandfather worked for a while as a scythe-man for local farmers, but later went to sea, serving as a stoker on a boat to Argentina. He met my grandmother at a dance in a house in Portally Cove and they set up home in the village of Dunmore East, close by the Protestant church and to some property owned by my grandmother's rich relative, Kathleen Harney.

On the night they met, Portally was a cove with many thatched houses set around it. Many of those living there remembered a time when Irish was the local language. Decades later, I went there. I went down a narrow road past some thatched houses and finally came to the cove. Ruined cottages could be seen here and there in the cliff-top fields. Small boats bobbed near the water's edge. I climbed a path through brambles and fern and, from a height, could see the grass grow greener in some parts of the fields. Those patches marked the site of cottages long ago deserted when their inhabitants emigrated to America or Newfoundland.

Years after I first went there, I heard a story about a woman who lived in a cottage in Portally and who never slept with her husband after their wedding-night. The story went that they got into bed and when she saw what he proposed to do next her mind turned with such terror that she refused to share a bed with him again. She had never thought such a thing possible. I saw her once on the road to Dunmore, her eyes haunted and demented as she walked with a bucket, an old woman with streaks of grey hair and an old overcoat. I was frightened and ran the minute I got around the next bend.

There was another old woman with grey hair that had once been red. My grandfather told me that, long ago, fishermen dreaded seeing her on their way to the boat because it was bad luck to go fishing after seeing a red-haired woman. Despite being a figure of bad luck, the old woman had kind, innocent eyes, and I never felt frightened when I saw her on the road or lighting a candle in the small convent chapel near the harbour.

Besides talking of fishing and the sea, my grandfather loved sport, especially hurling. Every Sunday, he turned on the wireless after our midday meal and arranged himself in the armchair near the fire. He placed a few bottles of stout on the floor next to his chair, on the arm of which he set a packet of Woodbines and a heavy silver cigarette lighter.

'Whisht now,' he would say when the match came on. The sound of the Artane Boys' Band playing the National Anthem blared through the kitchen. With a rusted brown bottle-opener, Grandad prised the top off a Guinness bottle. Sometimes, froth would foam over the neck of the bottle and he would let me lick it. I salvaged the bottle-tops from the floor and kept them.

As he listened to the match, Grandad held the stub of a pencil in one hand and a piece of white paper in the other. He wrote the names of the two teams along the top and when either scored he made a mark on the paper. A thick, heavy line meant a goal. A light line meant a point. By the end of the game, his sheet of paper was marked with lines until it looked like a drawing of stakes in a field, or like the lines cut into tally-sticks.

He became especially passionate when Waterford played. Once they were in the All-Ireland final against Kilkenny. Excitement gripped the house. The bottles were lined up beside the chair and the froth that settled in his glass eventually made an awkward moustache across his upper lip. Waterford lost the game, and he sat back in defeat once again as if it was a place he was well-used to.

In his late teens, my grandfather had joined the IRA in County Waterford. He stood on guard outside a cottage in the Nore Valley where Eamon de Valera held peace talks with Liam Lynch during the Civil War. He served in the Comeragh Mountains as a courier and came back one day to visit his mother in Knockapadden. From a distance, he could see a commotion around the house. Hiding, he looked down from a field high in the glen and saw a group of Black and Tans harassing his mother outside the house. To go any further would mean capture. Decades later, when former members of the IRA were presented with medals as a mark of their service, he turned down the offer. Fighting for Ireland, he said, was not something you did for medals.

My grandfather was not very comfortable in cities and never seemed completely at ease in the suburbs. Even the way he walked through the streets was different. Everything he did had a countryman's stamp to it and he adapted to a new environment by bringing his rituals with him like luggage. On Saturday nights, he went to the cupboard under the sink and took out tins of shoe polish, two brushes and some rags made from torn-up pyjamas. Polishing shoes was one of his rituals. His own were always shining. After myself and the others were dressed for bed, he took all our shoes and set them in a row. Then he polished them one by one, moving the brush through every corner and crevice. He left them for a while and then started the procedure again with a different brush, holding each shoe up before him as if he would not be satisfied until he could see the reflection of his own face in the leather. When the polishing was finished, he set the shoes down next to each other, and they were ready to be worn at mass the next morning.

'Sing me a rebel song,' he commanded. He liked the singing of the Clancy brothers, and when I got an Aran sweater like the group, he thought I really looked the part. I never heard him sing anything except a line or two of the 'Shoals of Herring'.

When he went away after the weekend, the smell of Guinness stayed around the house for most of Monday. Thin, sucked butts littered the fireplace. The bottles were gathered up and put into the corner of the coalshed where they lay for years. Cobwebs gathered about them and the labels peeled away.

In Dunmore East, my grandfather drank in a pub called Bill's. It was a dark pub full of fishermen. Sometimes, when we were staying in Dunmore, he took me in there on Sunday morning after mass. Then, he was dressed up in a suit and wore a clean cap. He was freshly shaved and his spotless white shirt gave a fresh look to everything he did. I drank lemonade as he poured out another large bottle of stout.

He was different in his own place. The city and our housing estate seemed to restrict him. In Dunmore, he looked through his window at the sea and the cliffs and, on a clear day, the Saltee Islands away in the distance. He was at ease on the road between his cottage and the harbour, or in the half-acre behind his cottage.

A shed behind the cottage held most of his tools and on sunny days he sat outside it on an upturned fishbox. 'Oh, be the hokey,' he said as he tried to mend a broken chair. He wore metal-rimmed glasses when doing any kind of close work. His mind became concentrated on the task and, if I said anything to him, he might not reply. On the wall of the shed behind him, I glimpsed a grey model Messerschmitt similar to those in the *Victor* comic I read every week. He never spoke much about the Second World War, except to say that on the day war broke out, in September 1939, he was just back from England. What he remembered most about that day was not the outbreak of war but the All-Ireland final at Croke Park, a match to which he hurried after getting off the mailboat at Dun Laoghaire. It was known as the thunder-and-lightning final.

My father had other memories of the war. On the wall of his house in Dunmore East, he pinned maps on which he traced the advances and retreats of armies across Europe. He saw the war in another way one day as he was walking along the cliffs and heard planes far out at sea. The two planes came closer and he saw that they were engaged in a dogfight, as a British plane fought against one of the German planes that sometimes flew along the coast and attacked British coal boats. The planes fought until both flew away and he never found out the result of the skirmish.

Otherwise, like my grandfather, he followed the course of the war in the pages of *The Irish Press*, a newspaper which the family, as de Valera supporters, bought every day.

My grandfather was at his most industrious in the garden. He had potatoes growing behind the house in drills that ran in the earth near the back windows. At the corner of the house stood a dark wooden barrel filled with rainwater that flowed from the gutter on the roof. I loved to watch the water in the barrel, hearing the quick plop of raindrops falling on the meniscus which reflected the sky and as much of my face as I dared to advance over the rim of the barrel.

There was water, too, in Glody's well. I walked there with my grandfather on mornings in August when my family went to Dunmore East for two weeks holiday. Grandad held two metal buckets with handles that squeaked as he walked. Straight ahead of us, the sea glistened. I could see the Hook Head lighthouse with its black-and-white circles. The night before, I lay in bed in the dark and counted the flashes of the lighthouse beacon spinning like a searchlight through the bedroom every six seconds. There was a smaller lighthouse in the harbour at Dunmore East and my grandfather had worked in it for a while. If I peered through its narrow windows, I could see a curling stairs with a golden banister.

Glody's well was behind a ditch just off the road. Its water was so clear that I sometimes had to strain just to see it. A pebble flicked into it caused a reaction as ripples shivered and spread to the walls, and it seemed as if the stones at the bottom shook. At evening, midges spun about the well in a hectic gauze. The clear surfaces of stones looked smooth and washed. When the bucket was put in, I had to force it down into the water and then it would suddenly start to sink, water pouring in as if the bucket was gulping. A full bucket was too heavy for me to carry but I kept my hand on the handle as my grandfather walked home, stopping awhile at a gate near the well to chat with Mrs Glody or her husband, Packie, who worked as a pilot in the harbour.

One day I was playing in the grass outside my grandparents' cottage when the atmosphere took on that change of tone I had learned to associate with danger. It was a tone I knew from the day my mother died. I went over by the steps leading to the front door and saw Grandad leaning on my father's shoulder. He had fallen and was trying hard to right himself. His sense of balance was completely gone and he could not stand. This was different to when he walked unsteadily after getting off the bus. This had a sinister feeling about it.

Shortly afterwards, he went into Ardkeen hospital in Waterford. One of his legs was amputated, a thought that terrified me. He came out of hospital just before Christmas and we went to Dunmore East to see him on Saint Stephen's Day. His three children were there — my father, Aunt Nancy and Uncle John. My grandmother had baked a Christmas cake; there were Christmas cards on the mantelpiece and on the old dresser in the parlour, but there was little sense of cheer in the house. My grandfather walked slowly on crutches up the narrow hall, trying to get used to a new sense of balance and weight. When I eventually mustered up the courage to look, I saw a thin trouser-leg where his leg had been.

A few days later he died. I was terrified of death in the family. Whenever anyone was seriously ill and the air seemed to hang heavily with imminent death, something inside me grew dark and closed.

A black car from the undertakers called to our house to bring us to Grandad's funeral. We got to the cottage in Dunmore East where scores of people were standing.

'Who are they now?' a man asked of a woman as we came in the gate.

'They're Richie's children from town.'

My father came to the front door. He wore a black tie with his suit. His eyes were red around the rims. 'Do you want to come in and say goodbye to Grandad?' he asked me.

'No,' I said nervously.

'Alright then. You four can go and wait in the car. I'll be with you in a minute.'

Our car took its place in a long line parked against the ditch outside the house. I recognised very few people: there was Mrs Glody and Packie; there was Mikey Toole, the milkman; there was Maurice Power, a fisherman, and Tommy Ivory, my grandfather's friend who tended the grounds of the Protestant church. Eventually the coffin was carried out. A tricolour was draped around it. Old fishermen and farmers blessed themselves. Leaning on my aunt's arm, my grandmother, who seemed to have become very small, came down the steps dressed in black. She wore a black mantilla on her hair.

The funeral wound down the hill towards the sea and made its way through the village, passing the harbour where my grandfather had worked, on past the Haven Hotel and the Protestant church, down into the lower village and then up a hill towards the church in Killea. He was buried there in a graveyard high above the sea. The headstones were marked with the names of people he had often talked about. Those names were so familiar to me that the graveyard seemed a small village in itself.

We went home to Waterford that night, but visited Dunmore East again the following weekend to see my grandmother. She was dressed in black and the house still had the feel of a funeral about it. Where there had been Christmas cards a fortnight ago, there were now sympathy cards and mass cards. My grandfather's wire-rimmed glasses lay on a shelf near his pension book. His box of shoe polish and brushes lay under the sofa. Three china pheasants flew across the wall above the fireplace.

When it was time for us to go home, we ran out to the gate and played in the gravel. Cones lay on the ground under a pine tree near the gate. We were waiting for Lynch's bus, an old bus, which had seen better days in England, trundling through the shires. On Sunday evenings it went all over the countryside collecting people for a bingo session in Waterford. It would stop at my grandmother's gate.

The bus came down the hill and my father put out his hand to indicate to the driver that he wanted to get on. As it slowed down, we said goodbye to my grandmother. Brendan, who was to continue living with her, played in the gravel near the gate. She was crying. Inside the bus, I rubbed away the mist on the fogged-up windows and looked out as a few others got on. I saw her wave and walk away towards the side of the house, where a few old fish-boxes were stacked. In her black clothes, she walked over the earth where my grandfather once had a vegetable patch. She walked up the half-acre and drew her cardigan closer about her. We waved from the bus, but she never looked back.

I stood at the edge of the Erin's Own Hurling and Football Club pitch and felt tension ripple through the crowd. A line of men stood in the goalmouth. They wore the club's blue and yellow jerseys. Around the pitch stood members of the Mount Sion team against whom they were going to play. The *sliotar* lay on a line a few yards away from the men in the goal-mouth.

Martin Óg Morrissey, wearing the blue and white Mount Sion jersey, held his hurley in one hand and rubbed the other against his hip, wiping away the sweat to improve his grip. He eyed the ball and measured the distance to the goalmouth where the line of men waited. The goalkeeper spat lightly onto his palms and rubbed them together. He pulled his cap down further on his head as the sun sank beyond the city. The crowd on the sideline leaned forward to get a better view.

The referee stepped back from the line where the ball lay, the whistle gripped in his mouth as he seemed to dance backwards. Morrissey, a burly man with dark hair, had a great reputation as a hurler and had played on the county team. He stepped forward and slipped his hurley under the *sliotar*. He tapped the ball into the air with a movement that was as deft as a dancer's and seemed incongruous from such a heavy man. I was standing near my father on the right-hand side of the goalmouth.

It appeared as if Morrissey gave the ball no more than a firm tap. There was a shuffle near the goal. Dust rose around feet. Men shouted. The ball was in the back of the net before Erin's Own even saw it. A cheer went up around the field. Any minute now, the referee would blow the final whistle and the game would be over. Morrissey had secured a Mount Sion victory.

Afterwards, my father took me into the dressing-room where the beaten Erin's Own players were changing. The room had a smell of sweat and grass; its whitewashed walls were cold to the touch. Hurling-boots lay on benches, the long laces dangling over the edge. Jerseys were crumpled on the ground. Paddy O'Connor, a friend of my father's and a member of the Erin's Own committee, collected the jerseys in a bag. He wore a soft hat. Like other members of the club, he was often in our house.

The Erin's Own club had known its greatest victories decades before I was born and long before my father moved to Waterford. Photographs of old teams and players were hanging on the walls of the clubhouse. Many of the surnames crossed generations as fathers and sons joined the club. There were Dowlings and Coadys and Wares. The Wares were legendary hurlers whose exploits were often discussed and embellished. Most of them were old when I saw them among the spectators at matches, but they stood with the confidence of men who knew what it was to be important.

My father went to a meeting of the Erin's Own committee every Monday night. When I was very young, Tessie would stay late that night. In time — when I was about nine — I could be trusted in the house and I liked the sense of having the place to myself when my father had gone out. Breda and Aidan went to bed and I made toast with a fork and bread held against a dying fire.

My father came in at half ten. He had the account books with him after the meeting; he was the club treasurer with responsibility for signing cheques and for counting money after the club's annual flag-day when young players stood with tins on streets around the city. The money was counted on the brown table in our sitting-room. It was poured from the tins and stacked in pennies, threepenny bits, half-crowns. A ten-shilling note was folded among the piles of copper coins.

My father was also involved with street leagues in John's Park. He had been a footballer himself when young, playing for Gaultier, a team formed of men who came from Dunmore East and its hinterland. One of the first photographs ever taken of me shows a baby set in a pram in the garden of my grandparents' house in Dunmore East. My grandfather's cap is on my head and a hurley lies next to me. I suspect that my father had high hopes of his sons becoming sportsmen. None of us did.

I was useless at hurling, but played nonetheless in the juvenile street leagues and became a sub for the Back Road team. My green jersey hung limply around me. Seldom given a chance to play, it was late in the game when I was finally told to run onto the pitch. I lacked the ability to forcefully crowd in on the ball no matter who was in sight and instead tended to look at other players, rather than at the ball. My hurley seldom connected properly with the *sliotar* that lay still in the grass as I pulled and whacked at it, missing it two or three times as the team mentors (my father among them) roared at me from the sidelines. 'Hit the bloody thing. Come on!'

'Jesus Christ, will you aim straight?' said someone else. By this time, the team from the Main Road had closed in and had taken the ball away in one easy movement. When the league was over, I was given a medal, but felt guilty about taking it. I had worked up no sweat to earn it, had scored no goals or shown even a hint of skill. I was taking the medal on false pretences and as a result it meant very little to me.

After leaving primary school in John's Park, I became interested in soccer. The Waterford soccer team was winning game after game. As they won, their support grew and the games in Kilcohan Park were drawing huge crowds. My father, like many GAA men, had no interest in soccer and was forbidden by the rules of the Gaelic Athletic Association to go to soccer games. Soccer was a foreign game. It was never played in school and, when a soccer team was formed by the pupils of Mount Sion, it was banned by the Christian Brothers. Hundreds of boys walked out in protest.

Sometimes I joined in soccer games around the street. The names of the England team in the 1966 World Cup became as well-known as the names of great hurlers had been to my father's generation. Running with the ball towards goalposts made of coats and jumpers, boys imagined themselves to be Bobby Charlton, Nobby Stiles or Geoff Hurst.

Gaelic football was another sport in which my father had an interest. He kept copies of the GAA annual, *Our Games*, on the sitting-room bookcase. He also kept the programmes from matches in a drawer in his bedroom, stacked together and sometimes taken out to settle an argument over a date or a result. The talk of hurling and football would go on for hours when one of his friends came to visit. Lying in bed upstairs, I heard them analyse games or sort out teams for forthcoming matches.

The names of players were written on special sheets before each game. Dates of birth had to be checked for juvenile games and most of the names were written in Irish. These sheets lay around the house, written out by my father, who used the old Gaelic script when he wrote the Irish names. I loved that script and had learned it myself during my first few years in primary school. After that, it was dropped and I used the same ordinary script whether writing in Irish or English.

The hurling club was my father's main social outlet. Most of his friends had some connection with it. Every year, he went to the club's annual dinner which was held in a city hotel. Once, he won the Clubman of the Year award, a statuette set among gold columns and imitation marble. His involvement in the sport also included writing brief notes on hurling for the *Waterford News and Star*. These notes had descriptions of games or news from the Erin's Own club. He wrote them on pages of my school copies, often using some phrase or description he had enjoyed in a national newspaper. 'The players were buzzing like bees around a honeypot — how does that sound?' he asked me. 'I have it down now anyway. It can stay in.'

When he bought the local paper on Thursday, the sports pages were the first he looked at and he was bothered if parts of the article had been cut. He included the names of all the players at the end of each match report and sometimes cut out the reports and kept them in his wallet.

My father's other main interest was horse-racing. Whenever I was in town with him, he took me into bookies' offices where he placed a bet. I would stand beside him in the crowded office as he listened to a radio commentary on a race. If the horse he had backed was beaten, he tore the docket in two, tutted, folded the two pieces of paper into a ball and threw them into a waste basket. The floor of the bookies' was strewn with crumpled dockets. If he won, he gave little indication of delight as he went to the counter to collect his money.

Race-meetings were sometimes held in Tramore and I went to them as well. They bored me since I was too small to see what was going on and I understood little of the process that began with a horse running and ended with my father's delight or disappointment. The excitement that gathered as the race progressed attracted me, but as usual a part of me held back from it while another part wanted to join in it fully. I stared around at people screaming and jumping, binoculars shaking against their chests and form-books held in their hands. Through the crowds, I could see the brief, bright flash of jockeys' silks.

On Sunday afternoons, major hurling and Gaelic football matches were held in Walsh Park near a suburb called Slievekeale. Walsh Park was also known as the Sports Field. My father lifted me over the turnstile and I ran ahead of him. Women stood behind tables and old prams stacked high with fruit and chocolates. Some of them sold flags and paper hats for one team or another. We were always for Erin's Own, always for Waterford. Country people crowded into the city for major games. Before the match, they sat on the grass eating sandwiches and drinking from flasks of tea, the sun beating down on them as a brass band paraded around the pitch.

The biggest games of all were the Munster final in Thurles and the All-Ireland in Dublin. My father went to these games without me. The All-Ireland was shown on television and I looked for his face in the crowd. When Waterford made it to Croke Park in 1963, the city went wild. They lost the game, but their homecoming was a triumphal procession. Brass bands welcomed the team at the railway station. The players stood on the back of a lorry that moved slowly along the quays and turned towards the Mall where I stood among the crowds. A platform had been set up outside the Town Hall. My father held me up and I saw the players wave from the lorry. Even though they had been beaten, it was a matter of pride for the crowd that they had made it at all.

Games defined groups of people in the same way as houses, or jobs or neighbourhoods. Schools had their own games. In the school in John's Park and in Mount Sion, hurling was the main sport. In Waterpark College, also run by the Christian Brothers, the boys played rugby. It was a posh school with which we had no contact.

I was never to share my father's fondness for sport and my interest as a participant diminished as time went on. I was happy to be a spectator, relishing moments like Martin Óg Morrissey taking a free or the tension as teams fought for winning scores with only minutes to go in a game.

The world of hurling was a seam running through our lives. It included the very names of teams — Erin's Own, Ballyduff-Portlaw, Brickey Rangers, Mooncoin — and the atmosphere of dressing-rooms and committee rooms where I sat waiting for my father. Its smells, its words, its sounds — the clatter of hurleys as two men tried to hit a ball at the same time; the roar of a crowd when a goal was scored — were patterns in the fabric of my days, and no matter how small my talent or how little my interest, it was as much a part of my life as the wallpaper in my bedroom or the broken teddy-bear whose glass eye stared out over the top of my wardrobe for years.

The Brother took the big roll-book from his desk and opened it. 'Settle down now lads,' he said. The shuffling stopped. He read out our names in Irish.

'Deasún Gloster—

Anseo— . . .

Seán Ó Duinn—

Anseo—

Annraoi Ó Floinn—

Anseo—

Seán Ó hÓgain—

Anseo—

I looked at the brown floor as the names were called out. Wooden tiles slotted into each other in a neat jigsaw. I started to count them, but gave up after thirty.

Rain pelted against the windows and the heat from the radiators fogged the glass. Through the fogged pane, I could barely see Mr Cunningham, the rent-man, heading for our road. Then the classroom door opened and a thin boy came in. He wore wellingtons and a heavy dufflecoat that was too big for him. His cheeks were red. The Brother closed the roll-book and looked at him.

'Ah . . . Jimmy O'Leary,' he said. 'You've decided to honour us by your presence, hah? And what's your excuse this morning?' He caught the boy's ear and started rhythmically to pull and push him away. The boy's face twisted in pain.

Jimmy O'Leary was always late. He lived farther from the school than the rest of us. His house was in the countryside outside John's Park, set just back from the road near a bridge where we sometimes went with jamjars in search of tiny fish.

He walked to school every morning, holding his two small brothers by the hand. I never saw him smile.

The Brother started to shout. 'No answer, hah?' He gave Willie a dig in the ribs. 'Take off your coat,' he ordered. The Brother took a leather strap from inside the black belt he wore around his soutane. He stroked his fingers with the strap as if testing its stiffness. The room went tense. 'This hurts me as much as it hurts you,' he said to Jimmy. Swishing through the air, the strap came down with a crack across the boy's outstretched hand. Once. Twice.

'Now, the other one,' said the Brother. 'Come on. Hold it higher. It's for your own good.' Jimmy raised his other hand and again the strap cracked twice. The Brother's face relaxed. Jimmy O'Leary's face grew twisted again and his eyes glassed over. He crossed his arms and pressed each sore hand against his ribs. 'Maybe tomorrow morning you'll be early,' said the Brother. The boy walked to his seat at the back of the class and the day's lessons started.

It was a large class with over forty boys. With a few exceptions, all our fathers worked in factories: the paper mills, the foundry, Clover Meats, the glass factory. Ronan Sheehy's father worked in an office. Des Gloster's father had been a teacher before he died.

'*Lámha trasna,*' the Brother would say when he wanted us to pretend to sleep, our eyes closed and our heads resting on folded arms. The Irish language was an important part of the school. *Leithreas* was the toilet where water gushed through the urinals. On cold and wet days, the floor became an ice-rink. I slipped once and banged my forehead on the floor, getting a large bump that never went away and over which I combed my hair.

Sos was the Irish for break-time. *Lón* was the Irish for lunch. *An Bráthar* was the Irish for the Brother. When the Inspector came he was called *An Cigire*. The greatest Brother of all was

An Bráthar Eamonn Iognáid Rís, the founder of the Irish Christian Brothers. We prayed daily for his canonisation. He had started teaching in Waterford in 1803, and for some years before that had worked as an apprentice to his uncle, a merchant who eventually left him his business. Edmund Rice aimed to educate the children of the deprived classes. He was buried in Mount Sion, the school to which many of us would go after leaving primary school. His body lay in a small mausoleum in the school grounds, surrounded by a concrete tomb with a narrow window in one side. It was possible to slide the glass back and knock at his coffin. I did this once and half expected a voice to say, 'Come in.'

In September, at the start of the school year, each class stood in straight lines in the playground. The teachers stood in a group, chatting and smoking. We sized them up as we stood, trying to work out which one we would get and sorting out the strict from the easy-going. Some classes were taught by lay teachers. Others got Brothers. Since the Brothers were in charge of the school, they had more power.

We also stood in the playground for P.E. or drill as it was called. A man from town, Mr Frazer, stood in front of us wearing a wine-coloured tracksuit (sometimes he stood on top of the shed) and made us perform repetitive exercises waving small red and green flags. This seemed to me a complete waste of time. I loathed it, just as I loathed the hurling matches held after school or on Saturdays. Standing with Des Gloster on the edge of the pitch, keeping as far away from the action as possible, I shivered and wished for the hurling match to end quickly. Since sport was high on the school's list of priorities, this attitude created problems of self-confidence and uncertainty.

While many of the teachers were kind and those who taught the younger children were especially gentle, there were others who ruled by a strict and violent code. With these teachers, the boys who were weakest at lessons were beaten more often than others. Most of the time I worked hard, though my aim was usually to avoid a blow rather than to know a lot. Once, I saw a teacher offer a boy a choice of the weapons with which he would be beaten. The teacher held his hands behind his back, with a stick in one and a strap in the other, and told the victim to choose.

Over the blackboard in every classroom, a statue of the Virgin Mary stood behind a glass cover. A vase of flowers was placed at her feet. Sometimes the flowers lay there for so long that they wilted, the water around their stems changing to a murky brown in which rotting petals floated. The Virgin's hands were joined in prayer and her eyes were raised to Heaven like the eyes of an exasperated teacher.

A few boys from the school became altar-boys in the Sacred Heart church, a parish church that was little more than a temporary ramshackle hut in the grounds of the nearby Ursuline Convent. Des Gloster was among the altar-boys and one Sunday, as I knelt at the altar-rails, I tugged at his cassock as he passed with the priest during communion. I was trying to make him laugh but he just stared at me. I felt contorted with guilt for weeks afterwards and eventually confessed to a bewildered priest that I had committed sacrilege. Shortly after that, the priest ran away and got married. That flummoxed me completely.

The class I liked best in school was that given over to the writing of English essays. I became absorbed in each essay and time seemed to fade away as I wrote, my mind and my pen becoming one as the words spilled out. Writing essays gave me a feeling that was the exact opposite of what I felt during games. At games, time passed slowly; when I wrote essays, it passed quickly. At games, I stood in anger; at essays, I sat in a trance.

My essays were long and adventurous, despite the predictability of the themes. One dealt with Saint Patrick on the Hill of Slane. Another told the story of a penny. Yet another told about Brian Boru, whose figure, as he knelt at prayer in his tent at Clontarf, was clear in my mind. The cruel Viking crept behind him and slew him savagely.

One of our history-books was a kind of comic called *Éire Sean's Nua*. Its message was simple: Irish good, English bad. Geography seemed mainly to be a list of towns and what was manufactured in them. Waterford had a glass factory and breweries. Our river was the Suir; our mountains were the Comeraghs. Dungarvan was the county town.

Religion was a catechism from which questions shot with the rapidity of a pub quiz. The catechism also had some coloured pictures, one of them showing a guardian angel preventing a boy from falling into a stream. There was a stream near John's Park and, when very young, I thought of its banks as places lined with rows of guardian angels waiting to stop us all from falling in.

I took part in school concerts and also played in the school's accordion band. After the last class every day, the monotonous sound of dated songs like 'The Rose of Aranmore', and 'The Moon Behind The Hill', sounded through the corridors and the surrounding streets, rising above the noise of the electric polisher pushed by Mrs Madigan the cleaner. Sometimes we played songs from the Eurovision Song Contest: 'Congratulations', 'Puppet On A String'. These were more like the songs we heard on the radio at home.

Brother Meagher was the last teacher I had in primary school. His nickname was Birdy. He had been a teacher in Mount Sion for years. Day after day, he fed us with more information than we had ever been given in all the years before. It was a regime under which the brightest became brighter and the dimmest faded away.

There was no remedial teacher in the school and boys who needed special help with reading never got the extra assistance they required. By the time they left school, their status was that of survivors whose relief was palpable.

The week before I left primary school, Birdy Meagher told us of what lay ahead. He spoke of secondary school and its subjects, of Latin and French and of the Latin words used at mass. I knew a few phrases like *Dominus vobiscum*, and *oremus*. On the left-hand side of the sixth-class blackboard, Birdy wrote Latin words. He wrote the word *mensa* (meaning table) and *puella* (meaning girl). Something happened to me as I saw and heard those words. It was as if the world had broadened. Language, opening like a calyx, was waiting for me to enter and claim it. The word *puella* went around in my head for hours, its liquid sound curling like the folds of a toga.

Birdy Meagher closed the roll-book on the last day. I went home and put my schoolbooks and copies into an old suitcase. My copies were all covered in left-over wallpaper from my sister's bedroom. At the start of every year, we were told to bring in the money for our new schoolbooks. If we left it too long, we were slapped. Then we were told to get our books covered. If we left that too long, we were punished again. Some parents wrapped the covers in brown paper bags. Most used wallpaper. One or two boys, who never seemed to do anything wrong and whose lives seemed to flow with a comfortable smoothness, used a better class of wallpaper than others to cover their books. Others had copies and books which in time looked grimy, neglected and in need of special care. These in their way reflected the circumstances of their owners, just as some had good strong schoolbags and others had tatty, worn ones.

I was learning that life had its own brutal pecking order and that those at the bottom would be kept there. I avoided the bottom but the impetus which kept me going was neither ambition nor love. At its most plain, with the exception of the English class, it was fear.

Jimmy O'Leary, the boy who was always late, left the school years before any of us. His family went away and I never saw him again.

After my grandfather's death, my grandmother Dunne came into town to stay with us more often. She changed the look of her cottage, giving it new wallpaper and paint, as if by changing the exterior world she could ease the sadness inside her as well. The garden out the back became a tangle of weeds, though I could still make out the ghostly rectangle of what had once been my grandfather's vegetable patch.

Her maiden name was Kathleen Cheasty and she came from Dunmore East. As a girl, my grandmother lived in a family that was sufficiently well off to send her to boarding school in Carrick-on-Suir, County Tipperary, but things started to decline when her father bought a pub in Dunmore East. Her mother was a beautiful-looking woman with clear skin, whose sepia photograph was framed on our sitting-room wall in John's Park. She died when my grandmother was a girl.

The pub teetered near the edge of a cliff in Dunmore East, not far from a ruined tower and overlooking a beach where waves whipped the walls in winter. I gathered from family gossip that my great-grandfather nearly drank as much as he sold in the pub, and there was always about my grandmother the feeling of someone who had once known better things.

Her marriage to my grandfather was not approved of by her family. Her cousin, Kathleen Harney, was the only close relative of hers' that I ever met. She seemed wealthy and owned a number of houses in Dunmore East, along with an orchard and a great many books. She had been educated at University College, Cork, and on the few times we met in her dark, antique-heavy house, I sensed an air of superiority and a desire for social complicity on grounds of education or wealth.

From my grandmother, I sensed the opposite. There was a pessimism about her that my father could display as well. This was a philosophy that held as one of its tenets the idea that very little would really go right. In every situation that seemed superficially good, there lay the germ that would make everything go wrong. My father's mother lived with an expectation of disappointment.

She liked books and was a member of two libraries: the Atlas Library on the Mall in Waterford and the small public library attached to Gertie Burke's grocery shop in Dunmore East. She read only one type of book: Mills and Boon romances. I often went with her to the library. As she scoured the shelves for new tales of love, I poked around in the children's section. She liked hospital romances and quickly read through books with covers that showed rugged doctors and fawning nurses. Everywhere she went, a Mills and Boon went with her and became part of a still life that composed itself on tables: her rosary; her black purse with a silver clasp; her mantilla for mass; a bottle of 4711 Eau de Cologne and, of course, the Mills and Boon.

She loved chocolate and was a terror for eating Rolos. Bits of gold wrapping-paper lay in flecks around the fireplace. Sitting by the fire in the evening after her day's work around the house in Dunmore East, she ate sweets and read love stories until she fell asleep.

Her chair, its seat covered in old red leather, had been in the family for decades. It was once the property of a relative who had been a famous priest. Father Cheasty belonged to that part of the family that had once known better days. He was buried in a grave at the side of Saint John's church in the centre of Waterford and my grandmother took me there to pray. As I stood at the grey kerb, I squeezed my eyes together and tried hard to pray for this man I had never seen and who had died decades before I was born. Someone told me that he had literally given away his shirt to a hard-up Waterford pauper.

Praying was a compulsive activity for my grandmother Dunne. God kept her going, just as he kept my other grandmother going as well. She was always at it. Church missions, novenas, First Fridays and benediction were all essential events to which I often accompanied her. My favourite was benediction with its Latin hymns and rattling chains around a censer, from which the smell of what I considered holiness was released.

She kept her missal near her, as well as the Treasury of the Sacred Heart and the latest issue of the *Sacred Heart Messenger.* Her prayer-books were stacked with more cards than a poker deck. There were memorial cards and cards with prayers for the conversion of sinners. There were cards showing Saint Martin de Porres and Our Lady of Lourdes. The Lourdes card, a memorial card for my mother, showed Mary balanced near a cleft in the rock above the young girl, Bernadette Soubirous, who knelt and looked up at the apparition poised in a swirl of pale roses and wispish clouds.

'Your mother was very fond of the Little Flower,' my grandmother told me. My mother's old prayer-book, which I frequently examined in a rage of self-pity and loss, had cards in it as well. One showed Saint Thérèse of Lisieux, the Little Flower, standing in her Carmelite habit and holding a bunch of flowers. Her face was smooth-skinned and block-like. She had died young, like my mother, and sometimes in the midst of all these cards and prayers and death, I felt a sense of decay and morbid languor from which I badly wanted to get away.

Pope Paul VI was my grandmother's hero. On Christmas Day, he appeared on television to deliver his *Urbi et Orbi* message to the world. My grandmother, staying with us in Waterford, stopped basting the turkey and sat down to watch. Then, when the time came for the Pope to impart his blessing, she shuffled in her seat. Turning in his heavy vestments, the Pope's raised hand moved in a slow half-circle above the crowds in Saint Peter's Square. He intoned the Latin blessing and my grandmother knelt down on the kitchen floor.

'Kneel down and get the Pope's blessing,' she told me. I put my toy to one side and knelt down. The lino was warm against my bare knees. I joined my hands. She nudged me. 'Bless yourself now.' I crossed myself slowly in time to the Pope's stately voice. A camera closed in on his face and I saw the Pope look my grandmother in the eye. She bowed her head. Out of the corner of my own eye, I saw my new toys lying on the table. I finished blessing myself as a great cheer rose from the crowds in the Vatican. My grandmother and I stood up.

'The Pope is a lovely man,' she said. 'I'm very fond of him.' I did not like him all that much. I preferred the last Pope, John XXIII, who had more Roman numerals after his name and who was known as Good Pope John. When he died, photographs of his corpse appeared in the newspapers. His still, round face haunted me. I imagined him as darkness fell and was terrified of looking into my father's room at night in case I saw Pope John's ghost on the bed. I knew nothing about him except that Mass was now said in English instead of Latin as a result of his ideas.

Kneeling down in front of the television made me feel uncomfortable and vaguely ridiculous. In future years, I made a point of disappearing before *Urbi et Orbi* started. It was never that simple, however, since the blessing was shown on the news later that night and my grandmother went through the rigmarole once again. Kneeling down in front of the news seemed an even stranger thing to do.

I preferred going to the pictures with her. Sometimes, on summer evenings, she took me walking into town. 'It's too nice to get a bus,' she said. 'The walk will do you good.' I liked to walk with her through streets that had a tea-time quietness about them. She spent ages looking at clothes or shoes in shop windows and this part bored me beyond measure.

She bought two packets of Rolos before going into the Savoy cinema. With her, I saw *Red River* and various versions of Jesse James's story. Cowboy films were her favourite. She chewed her way through them, peeling away paper from the packet of Rolos and placing a sweet in her mouth without once taking her eyes from the screen.

Her hands changed as she grew older. She had small hands into which deep lines were cut, and the skin became loose and wrinkled as she aged. A wedding-band circled one finger. When she baked soda bread, her hands were covered in flour and, after washing them, the knuckles were creased with lines of caked flour that she scraped away with a fingernail.

There was no running water in her cottage and eventually a tap was fixed to a wall in the front garden. Every year, when we stayed with her on holidays, she washed me at this tap on Saturday night. She put a plastic basin, the smell of which I hated, on a chair and filled it with warm water, then poured shampoo on my hair and dug her hands against my skull, working up to a lather that stung my eyes. I grimaced.

'What kind of man are you at all?' The cold went through me. She forced my head under the tap and held it there as freezing water gushed and washed the shampoo away. She towelled my hair dry, her fingers kneading my head. 'Hurry now and get your shirt on,' she said, 'or you'll catch your death.'

My grandmother never seemed too sure of her place in the world, but she was certain that the world's benefits were mainly for others. When she was younger, she had lived in suspicious fear of those she called 'the gentry'. These seemed to include all Protestants. 'When I was a girl,' she told me, 'if you were a Catholic walking through the village and one of the gentry came along, you had to get out of their way to let them pass. If you didn't, some of them would lash out at you with a walking stick. The men had to touch their caps if one of the gentry was going past and you'd think some of the caps would be worn away from the men touching them so often.'

Since Brendan lived with her in Dunmore East after my mother died, she was especially strict with him. She taught him manners and hygiene and was never slow to criticise if he slipped up on either count. Her standards were rigid where prayer, morality and modesty were concerned. To take off your clothes in front of others before a bath amounted to immodesty. Getting ideas above your station was a sign of 'notions'. These were all-encompassing and included everything from big words and lipstick to posh houses and difficult books.

In this way, my grandmother's disdain kept those around her in their place in much the same way as her hairnets kept her curls in order. She had started out in a world secure and full of promise but the early death of her mother and her father's wayward drinking had introduced her to life's hurtful ways.

With my grandfather, who was sometimes away on boats for months at a time, she built a life and a family. After his death, that too was gone and there was only the thought of him as she looked into the fire at dusk. A few times, I overheard her talking to him as if he was still alive. Nothing answered back except the sound of a broken-up fishbox burning in the grate.

'Santa Claus is in the paper,' said my father when he came in from work. He had the *Evening Press* in his pocket, rolled up like a baton with the racing pages on the outside. I took the paper, the name of which was written in white against a mauve square on the front page, and spread it out on the floor. The broadsheet pages were too big to hold in my hands.

I knelt on the floor and scanned the pages. Finally I found him: Santa Claus on a page of advertisements. A fat and jolly cartoon, he waved a bell as reindeer flew through the sky behind him. Stars were scattered around him. His photograph was on another page and showed him giving out presents in a street in New York.

When Christmas was on the way, my father drew up a list of annuals. We got comics every week: *Victor*, *Topper*, *Beano*, *Dandy* for the boys; *Bunty* or *Judy* for Breda. For Christmas we got an annual, the book of the comic. My father ordered the annuals in Kennedy's, a small shop in Johnstown, close to the Waterford Glass factory near the centre of town. It stood between a chip-shop and a tiny sweetshop owned by a friend of Tessie's who also sold cooked pigs' feet wrapped in newspapers.

Sometimes I went with my father into Kennedy's. Comics and newspapers were piled everywhere. Magazines lay on racks near shelves of sweets and cigarettes. We picked out the annuals, four in all, and every Friday after that my father called in on his way home from work and paid a fixed amount towards their cost. The last payment was made on the Friday before Christmas.

Of all the presents we got, annuals and books were the ones

that lasted the longest. I read them over and over, long after toys were broken or forgotten. Even their smell excited me. To open a new annual and hold its pages under my nose satisfied me as much as reading the stories. I often fell asleep as I read and the smell of an annual met me the minute I woke up, the pages open on the pillow.

The *Victor* annual had many war stories. Breda's annuals were different and I read them as well with their stories of girls' schools and orphans forced to work as skivvies in Victorian households. The boys' comics had German words in stories set during the Second World War: *achtung, donner und blitzen, heil*. There was also an athletics story I liked very much, *The Tough of the Track*, telling of a working-class athlete whose usual diet was fish and chips (or a one-and-one as he called it) and whose attitudes were permanently unconventional. A fish-and-chip van parked in our street on Fridays and I could imagine him standing in the queue there.

The Christmas tree went up in the sitting-room a week or so before The Great Day. A lorry drove around the streets stacked with pine trees and my father picked one to suit our low-ceilinged sitting-room. This was a room that really came into its own at Christmas. We hardly used it the rest of the year. It held a large brown table and some brown chairs with leather seats. A photograph of my father and mother on their wedding-day was hanging on one wall. It showed him sitting in a chair while she stood beside him. In her left hand, she held a missal which now lay in a drawer in my father's bedroom. It had a mock marble binding and a mock gold chalice set inside the front cover. The paper was thin and ribbons marked pages here and there. The parts of the ribbons that dangled outside the pages were a darker colour to those that lay within. The sides of the pages were smooth when I drew my finger across them.

The sitting-room was where I practised my accordion

for the school band. It was also the room where my father took visitors from the Erin's Own hurling club. But Christmas was the only time the sitting-room developed a feeling of being lived in. The fire was lit and the floor was soon covered in wrapping paper and half-empty bottles of Sullivan's lemonade.

Our Christmas tree had no lights. Looking out of the bedroom window at night, I could see lights flashing on and off on trees in some other sitting-rooms in the street. That seemed fancier. A few houses had artificial trees, but most, like ours, had real ones. The smell of the tree filled the house. It was a smell of forests and wooded paths like those I ran across in Dunmore East. It was a scent of the countryside and it took over the rooms, mixing in my mind with the excitement of minerals and cards and crackers. On top of the tree, a crooked fairy leaned forward with her wand. Every year, my father went to Woolworths and bought glittering balls and frosted baubles to hang on the tree. At least one would break, its splinters scattered among fallen pine needles.

As Christmas Day approached, more and more cards came through the letterbox. I set them up on shelves among pieces of crockery and delft, which included a porcelain pair of Georgian lovers in a bower. A few cards stood on the brown wireless from which the tinny music of 'O'Donnell Abú' was emitted as Radio Éireann came on the air every morning. The cards came from the same people every year: Aunty Bessie and family; Mattie and Violet and the children; John and Lily; Seán and Peggy; Nana and Brendan; some from relatives we hardly ever saw. One came from Mayor Richard Daley of Chicago, addressed to The Dunne Family, Waterford, Ireland. We left it in a prominent position on the shelf for days, but it turned out to have been for another family altogether. For a moment we felt touched by great events, but that it should not be for us seemed to my grandmother to be part of an inevitable pattern.

My father always posted Christmas cards at the last minute. He sent them to those who had already given us cards. He usually bought Irish-made cards with verses by Mai O'Higgins and with Celtic designs on the cover. These were dearer than other cards and invariably he would never have enough of them. Then, one of us was sent down to O'Regan's shop to buy a few cheap cards that were run-of-the-mill in their design. They showed robins in the snow against a background of silver bells, or thin magi on camels against a starry sky.

In the week before Christmas, carol-singers went through the streets nearly every night. They called at each door and collected money for charities like the Saint Vincent de Paul Society or the Good Shepherd Convent. Once, a group from the Protestant Cathedral went slowly around the estate on the back of a lorry. They held lanterns and sang carols I had never heard before. I knew no Protestants and only one such family lived in John's Park. They seemed a different people. When a new church opened just outside John's Park, a choral group put on Handel's *Messiah* there and many Protestants went along. I went as well. The Protestants had different accents. They carried cushions which they settled on the pews. This seemed a sensible idea, though it was one which made me feel a little guilty since we had been taught that comfort could be a sin and hardship was a good thing in the eyes of God.

Nana and Brendan came in from Dunmore East on Christmas Eve, along with my grandfather in the years before he died. Aunt Bessie came and always brought a cake with a tiny Santa Claus perched on top. She held a stack of parcels which included a compendium of games.

Aunt Nancy called and gave presents of tea-towels. Mrs Dowling, whose family were involved in the Erin's Own club, sent a Christmas pudding. One Christmas Eve, after a strike in the paper mills, a mysterious parcel of food arrived. Its source was never revealed.

There was also the paper mills party, an annual event for the children of workers in the factory. The party was held in the ITGWU hall in town and I usually ended up singing a song there, my mouth too close to the microphone and my voice sounding more like a boom than a melody as I belted out 'I'll Tell My Ma.'

Aidan and I went to the party wearing Aran sweaters which Tessie had knitted for us. 'You look just like the Clancy Brothers now,' she said. We stood at a microphone to sing together, but the song quickly became a battle as I shoved him away and he tried to squeeze back. We pushed and shoved — or rather, I pushed and he shoved — and the song came across as a very uneven duet.

My grandmother gave us all a bath on Christmas Eve. Breda walked down the stairs to the bathroom. She had nothing on and received a stern lecture about modesty. 'You can wear your new rig-out tomorrow,' my grandmother said. Rig-out was one of her special words that I never heard used by anyone else. She called tablecloths 'oilcloths', a word I never managed to fit to its object.

After we were washed and dressed for bed, we heard a radio programme from the North Pole in which Santa Claus greeted the children on whom he was going to call that night. We went to bed and I stood at the bedroom window looking out at the dark sky, searching for a flicker near the moon or the sudden glint of a sleigh among the stars. I breathed on the windowpane and wrote my initials on the foggy patch. From downstairs, the smell of cooking rose as my grandmother prepared a huge ham.

When I was a little older, she took me to Midnight Mass on Christmas Eve. I held her hand tightly as we walked through the streets. It was the latest I had ever been up, but I felt alert. We went down a street facing a field at the back of the school. At the far side of the field, a wall marked the boundary with Saint Otteran's psychiatric hospital. Every now and then, rumours went around the streets that a madman had 'escaped from the Mental,' and he had been seen in back gardens at night.

On Christmas Eve, the mental hospital looked like a ship lit up. I had never seen it in the dark before. Lights glowed in its many windows and its red bricks were now a dim grey. I trembled nervously as I looked at it. On summer days, rows of patients worked in drills outside it: quiet men with staring eyes, women with lurid red lipstick across their mouths and with short, straight hair. At Christmas, I imagined them wandering in their rooms, moaning and sighing under ceilings where paper decorations were pinned by voluntary workers and the Jimmy Atkins band played dance tunes.

We went past Doyle's shop and got closer to the new church. I had been too young to go to Midnight Mass in the old church. The church was packed and still had a smell of newness about it. The choir sang carols. Going home afterwards, tiredness took over and Christmas morning seemed far away as time became jumbled in my head.

Before going to bed, I looked in the sitting-room for a moment. The turkey was trussed on a plate, ready to go in the oven next morning. A few bottles of stout lay under the Christmas tree. The cooked ham was placed next to a box of Jacob's assorted biscuits. There was a box of Lemon's sweets with a large Santa Claus on the wrapping. I closed the door and went up to bed, too tired even to think of what might be happening in the night sky.

When we got up next morning, the rooms were still very dark. We piled onto my father's bed and within minutes the bedroom was a chaos of wrapping-paper and boxes: Ludo,

Snakes and Ladders, a game of draughts, selection boxes with various sweets and bars of chocolate, Dinkies, annuals, dolls for Breda, jigsaws. I got a large yellow bulldozer which made me so excited I ran down the stairs to show my grandmother. Halfway down, it fell from my hand and landed on my bare big toe. I screamed with pain.

One Christmas morning, when I was seven, I got, for the first time, a book with no pictures. It was a red-covered copy of *Tom Sawyer* and was given to me by my father's brother, Uncle John. My father gave me *Tales of Brave Adventure*, a book of stories about Robin Hood and King Arthur. Told by Enid Blyton, its illustrations included a picture of a hand surfacing in a lake. The hand gripped a sword. It was an image at which I could look for a long time, imagining the waters of the lake rippling as a hand broke through them from an underwater world.

One Christmas Eve, in a year when childhood was nearly over, I had a cold and my grandmother decided that hot whiskey was the only thing to cure it. My father never drank alcohol. My grandmother never drank it either and had no idea of how potent a small amount of whiskey could be. I lay in bed sweating. My pyjamas became clammy and stuck to my skin. Hot lemonade, my father's usual cure, seemed too mild when measured against the ferocity of my fever. 'I'll make you up a hot whiskey,' my grandmother said. 'They say it's very good for the flu.'

She came up to the bedroom with a large glass filled to the top. Cloves swam in it and grains of sugar settled at the bottom. I drank it down quickly and fell asleep in no time. The following morning my head felt as if someone was inside it hammering at the skull. I thought this was just a symptom of serious flu.

By the time we sat down to Christmas dinner every year, my grandmother was flustered. She had been cooking all morning. The heat from the oven warmed the kitchen where a huge fire blazed. We moved between there and the sitting-room. Once, the walls of that room were spattered after an experiment I conducted with a toy chemistry set for which I was years too young. A test tube, in which a dozen substances were mixed and shaken and heated over a burner, had exploded with a force that both frightened and delighted me. Luckily, the wallpaper in the sitting-room was off-white and it was some time before my father noticed the scores of tiny white stains.

Out in the street, boys and girls could be seen on the footpaths showing off their new bicycles or toy prams. Girls stood with new dolls and brushed wispy black or yellow hair with small toy brushes. Boys pushed vehicles along the paths and waited for sparks to come out as engines whirred.

On Christmas night, a photographer went from house to house. We posed for a photograph: my father, and his four children. I wore short pants and sat at the edge of the sofa, my hands on my knees. Later, my father and grandmother watched television while we stayed in the sitting-room. I felt sick and burped continuously from the effects of Sullivan's lemonade, empty bottles of which lay around the room, one or two with broken biscuit crumbs set sloppily around the rim. I was always too full or sick to eat at teatime on Christmas day and I turned away from the small plates of cold turkey. I picked at the cake and pudding which followed. 'No wonder you're only skin and bone,' my father said.

On Saint Stephen's Day the world was back to its old form, dispelling the illusion that reality had changed. The milkman from Snowcream Dairies went around again and the first sound I heard was the engine of his van trundling through the cold streets. Glass bottles clattered on doorsteps. Sometimes I saw birds pecking at the red and silver bottle-tops. The top of the bottle held cream and there was always a fight at breakfast over who got to pour it on their porridge.

My father remembered wren boys going around the countryside on Saint Stephen's Day, but we never saw any. He sang part of a song about the wren, the king of all birds, on Saint Stephen's Day got lost in the furze. I knew a story about how the wren had hidden in the feathers of an arrogant eagle and when the eagle flew as high as he could, the wren rose from his back and thus ascended even higher to become the king of the birds. Otherwise, the wren meant nothing to me. I knew it was small, but would not recognise one. I knew what a robin looked like because I had seen them on Christmas cards and sometimes in the street. I knew swallows because they gathered on the electricity wires outside our house before flying to Africa. Otherwise, I knew nothing about birds except that their shit was white.

On the evening of Saint Stephen's Day, we went to Aunt Bessie's house for tea. I liked it there. I picked out the melodies of Christmas carols on the piano or listened to my red-haired cousins play. Elizabeth, a cousin about the same age as myself, liked big words as much as I did. She and her friends would stand like angry teachers and say: 'Are you insinuating that I should tolerate such insolence from a human specimen like you?'

My aunt took out her best china and we drank from thin cups set on thin saucers. She called me Johnnymeboy and laughed. I was pleased that she was my godmother. I felt safe in her house where there always seemed to be plenty of food and where a row of brown wooden pipes, which had belonged to my maternal grandfather, was set on a wall in the sitting-room, each of them in a hole on a brown wooden rack with a hunting scene over it and a line about John Peel cut into the wood.

Aunt Bessie had a magazine rack near the piano and I spent ages looking through it as adults talked in the kitchen and the other children played in the hall. The rack held old copies of the *Munster Express*, the *Word*, *Pioneer*, and leaflets from the Saint Joseph's Young Priests Society. My aunt was very religious and sometimes, when I visited her house at night, I found that I had arrived at the time when everyone knelt down to say the rosary in Irish. We recited the rosary in my house as well, though we prayed in English and said only one decade. We knelt before the fire every night, my father and the three of us with Brendan if he happened to be with us, and said our prayers. We always said the same thing at the end: 'God bless Nana, Grandad, Daddy, Breda, Brendan, Aidan and Seán, and Holy God make Mammy happy in Heaven.' It was like a song.

By the time our Christmas visit to my aunt's was over, we were stuffed with food and lemonade again. Our pockets were padded with presents from crackers: plastic whistles, bits of white paper with riddles and jokes, paper hats. If one of our relatives with a car was visiting, we got a lift home; otherwise we walked. My aunt lived in Roanmore in the top part of the city and we made our way home down Bunker's Hill or by Hennessy's Road. The city seemed very big then, spread out below us like a carpet of lights onto which we were about to step.

The night was cold but I felt warm inside after the comfort of my aunt's house. With her cabinets of fine crockery and her carpeted floors, her polished furniture and her china cups, she seemed part of a different world. When I got home, I went to bed and started reading *Tom Sawyer*. The light from the street-lamp outside my window cut through a slit in the curtains and shone on the wallpaper, where teddy-bears and golliwogs stared and brown flecks marked the spots where, in the excited, sleepless nights, Aidan and I had torn away tiny pieces of paper and watched them flutter slowly to the ground.

The post mortem on my mother's body showed that she had died of heart failure. Traces of tuberculosis were found in her lungs. Her family, the Walshs, had been ravaged by TB and some of her brothers and sisters had died from it. Tuberculosis ran riot in many families in Ireland and my mother's would not have been unusual in this regard. In fact, by the sheer scale with which it tore through the family, her home was a typical testament to the power of a disease that some saw as an Irish leprosy.

After my mother's death, four children were still alive in the Walsh family. The others — I never knew how many but it was a very large family — had all died when young. It was the custom in Waterford that when a member of a family died, the men who remained would wear a black diamond patch on the sleeves of their jackets for some time afterwards as a sign of mourning. My grandfather Walsh became known around the city as a man whose children were dying in such numbers that the black patch never left his sleeve. His children died one after another, and in 1959 he died himself. My mother died the following year.

In the same way, my grandmother Walsh wore a black scarf and coat to signify her long bout of mourning. I only saw her when taken to her house on visits. She died in 1963, when I was seven. A small woman with a crinkled neck and dark hair, she lived in a terraced house in Griffith Place. The rooms were heavy with the genteel smell of furniture polish and lavender. Dried flowers were set in a heavy vase. The crisp petals cracked and broke when I touched them. The white ones were called Honesty, she said.

Grandmother Walsh came originally from Carrick-on-Suir in County Tipperary. My grandfather came from the same town and they moved to Waterford where he set up a tailoring business in Michael Street. He was a musician too, one of those who could pick up an instrument and master it quickly. This was a gift he passed on to his children and, as I found out in time, to myself as well. One of his brothers was also a musician and was known around Carrick as Tatter Jack Walsh.

My grandfather ran the Premier Dance Band and some of his children accompanied him as he played. They played in country dancehalls and in small hotels around County Waterford. They also played in the Savoy cinema, entertaining the audience between films, or for seaside crowds in the dancehalls in Tramore.

My mother went to school in the Presentation Convent at Slievekeale. During her summer holidays, she cycled with her sisters and friends to Tramore or Dunmore East. After one such trip, she wrote a poem about Tramore and it was published in a school magazine. I never learned much about her girlhood or even about her family. Most of what I knew I deciphered from photographs, like that which showed her sister, Anna, who had died from TB at the age of nineteen in 1949. Dark-haired and neatly-dressed Anna stood at the doorstep in Griffith Place, her hand resting against the porch as if to imitate the hand of a Hollywood star resting against a mock-Roman pillar. She was beautiful.

The Walshs were regarded as a religious family. The boys were well-mannered and the girls dressed modestly. Facing so many deaths strengthened my grandmother's religious outlook. It was religion that made sense of the suffering she witnessed as she watched many of her children become ill and waited for the harsh cough which indicated that yet another child was soon to die. Suffering was at the very heart of Catholicism: it was a prelude to redemption and so, despite everything, it had a purpose. God's will was an impenetrable force that would explain everything in the end. My grandmother sat in the pews of the new Ballybricken church near her home and found, in the flickering candles, familiar statues and beeswax smell, and in the pages of her prayer-book, a solace that life could not otherwise offer. When she took me into the church, I knelt beside her as she buried her face in her hands.

A banjo was fixed to the wall over the mantelpiece in her living-room. The room held a piano as well. Against the daily effort to tend a family, music rose as a celebration and escape. Tailoring was not a lucrative business, so the extra money made by the musicians was welcome in a house where a large family made huge demands on food, money and clothes. As a result of my grandfather's tailoring skills, the children were always well turned-out.

In some inarticulate way as I grew up, I made an equation in my mind concerning the two sides of my family. The Walshs seemed urban, sensitive, musical, spiritual. The Dunnes seemed physical, rural, political, and sports-loving. Later I realised that this equation was simple-minded and unfair, but at the time it suited me to believe in it. Depending on my mood, I would choose between the two and would most often come down on the Walsh side. I set the two at odds with each other in my mind, as if they were dogs thrown into a pit. My father, for example, was unmusical. My mother, by the same token, had no interest in politics and had seldom even looked at the many newspapers my father took into the house.

As I grew and found it easier to play an accordion than to wield a hurley, and discovered that the story of Tom Sawyer could move and excite me, I created in my mind a fictional portrait of my mother as someone who would have understood me perfectly and whose permanent absence therefore put me at a loss. This may have been true, though it could only have been partly true since her absence intensified those parts of my personality by which I felt closest to her. Had she still been alive, I would have accepted these things in the usual way and would have had no reason to use them as excuses for intense retreat and self-absorption. It was her death that made me what I was.

I created a particular atmosphere around my mother's family. They were very different from my father's. Where his landscape was a view of fields and the sea, my mother's family lived in a landscape of streets with names like Spring Garden Alley and Roanmore Park; of lanes, shops and small gardens. My two maternal aunts and two uncles lived in the city, all within walking distance of the town centre.

One of my uncles, Seán, worked as a printer; another, Mattie, worked in the jute factory near my grandmother's house in Griffith Place. Mattie was visiting our house in John's Park one day when he picked up the battered accordion I played in the school band. It was some years since he had played any instrument but his fingers flitted across the keys with the airy lightness of an expert. I saw for an instant the skill with which he once would have played, and I felt as well the way music became a thing in itself, its power fed by the grief of the everyday but transcending it as well.

Bessie and Delia were my mother's two surviving sisters and each was a frequent visitor to our house. I loved to see them arrive. Bessie had the biggest influence upon me and, in some ways, she took on my mother's role. In much the same way as her black bicycle with its wicker basket had been outside the door in the days before my mother died, she was to stay close to my life.

She had been a widow since the early death of her carpenter husband, my Uncle Jimmy, who died after he became ill one evening in Barrack Street. He had made our kitchen table and a crenellated wooden castle which was one of my favourite toys. Bessie paid for my schoolbooks and was forever impressing upon me the importance of education as a way of bettering myself. Ceaseless study was the road to getting on. Her own son, Dick, who was older than me, seemed locked in his bedroom surrounded by schoolbooks and homework.

When free education was introduced in 1965, she saw the path ahead with a new freshness and clarity. My father was different in this regard since, while he was anxious that each of us try hard at school, he was not overtly pushy about it either. Like many of the boys in his class at Killea national school near Dunmore East, he had left at the age of thirteen. He had been a bright pupil, but neither money or circumstances existed for him to go any further in school. He seldom spoke of his school-days and the only such references he made had to do with some old schoolfriend, or with the subcutaneous air-cells of a certain gull he had studied for a school project. 'Sub-cutaneous,' he said. 'There's a word for you.'

When the time came for me to attend secondary school, my aunt encouraged me to think of going there. In time, I became the first person in my father's branch of the Dunne family to sit the Leaving Cert exam — a situation that would bring its problems as well. The fees for secondary school education had been prohibitive, but changes in the system now meant that everyone who wanted to could attend secondary school and, with the help of a scholarship, go on to university. This was the path I would take eventually take, along with a number of my friends, and it was an unknown territory for all of us.

Since books held me in thrall, it was natural that my aunt should encourage me in school. I was useless at sports and, like all poor sportsmen, blamed sport instead of myself. I was useless at anything that demanded physical prowess or dexterity and what little skill I sometimes showed at sport came from cuteness rather than natural ability.

It was the same with crafts. My Aunt Bessie gave me a toy carpentry set for Christmas when I was eight but the results were so disastrous that she vowed never to give me such a gift again. My mental ability became a frequent topic of discussion and it was decided that, whatever about anything else, I had brains to burn.

My problem was one of application. I had no interest in being the best at anything in school; I found that I could learn things quickly but I lacked the patience needed to master them. It was the same with music: I had no trouble in learning to play an instrument, but felt no desire to read music or to study the finer points which make the difference between competence and excellence.

My taste in music was old-fashioned. Besides the ballads and rebel songs I sang for my grandfather in the years before he died, and the songs I learned from Tessie and from the songsheets she gave me, I liked listening to classical and traditional Irish music on the radio. This created a problem: classical music was considered the taste of a snob; to like it was a symptom of what my grandmother Dunne would have seen as 'notions'. So I made it into a part of my other, inner world — that other place to which I retreated when angry, distant or inexplicably upset. The music of the Beatles, Cliff Richard and the Rolling Stones was forever on the radio during the day, but the stern resonance of a cello and violin had a deep attraction which no amount of disdain could dissipate.

I decided to learn the violin and a teacher in school loaned me an instrument. I stood before the mirror that was fixed to the inside of the door of my father's wardrobe and imagined myself playing before an audience of thousands, drawing the smooth bow over the strings and hearing sweet music emanate from the depths of the instrument. All that actually could be heard was a series of harsh and ugly shrieks.

I met the music teacher and she said I could never play the violin properly: my left-handedness made it impossible and the instrument was given back. I looked at my left hand as if it was suddenly an immense handicap that would have to be chopped off, and decided instead to play the accordion and the tin-whistle, the mouth organ and the recorder. When in my aunt's house, I played the piano and found no difficulty in picking out the melodic lines of simple tunes. My aunt patiently said nothing as I searched the keys for new songs and never went any further than the melody, the complexities of the left-hand keys eluding me.

Bessie spoke frequently of my mother, to whom she had been very close. I tried to tease memories from her. To hear someone talk of my mother could give me thought for days. It also presented me with images to which I held as if they were driftwood for a stranded islander. A neighbour told me how she remembered my mother wheeling a pram along the footpath with myself and Aidan piled in it. I nursed that image for hours, trying to make it stronger and more real until I felt it fade away like all the others.

Another neighbour, Mrs Meehan, with whose son, Gerard, I often played, told me one evening of her work as a nurse. My father sent for her whenever any of us became ill. She put bandages around many of our cuts and grazes and told me of how she had come to the house just after my mother died, and of how my mother looked then, young with all the life gone out of her. I was having my tea in Mrs Meehan's house as she told me this and suddenly felt seized by a sense of terror. I fixed my attention on a jar of Rose's lime marmalade in the centre of the table and then stared at a carton of Saxa salt. I bit my tongue. Then I burst into uncontrollable laughter. It was a hysterical act and the image of my mother lying dead on the bed in the room where I imagined ghosts at night was too much to bear.

Yet my mother's family seemed a family of ghosts, of lives spent with suffering and drawn into death when young. From my remaining aunts and uncles, I drew memories until it seemed the Walsh family were completely set in the past, like my mother's book of black-and-white photographs of filmstars. In that book, Clark Gable, Mae West, Betty Grable, Marilyn Monroe, Gregory Peck and dozens of others looked out, their showy signatures penned across the margins or against the folds of a flamboyant gown.

In the same way, the world of my mother and her lost brothers and sisters was an old book I kept in my mind. As I looked at old photographs or listened to my relatives talk of the past, it never struck me that if I let go of the mood which came over me at such moments I might find myself as I really was in the shadow of what stayed behind. Instead, I held onto other people's memories of the dead and hugged them close to me, as if by letting go I would find, terrifyingly, that there was nothing left behind only a dark and bottomless space beyond comfort and care.

For my mother's family, the countryside was a place to visit. When they spoke of it, the place-names had an air of roads shadowed by trees and of fields past which they cycled like tourists. They spoke of Dunhill, Annestown, Mooncoin, the Five Cross Roads, and of walking past the Yellow House, a shop at the edge of the city on the Cork road, as if all these places marked an area filled with sights for summer visitors. The natural world was seen in terms of fields or the sea or country roads, never in terms of animals, plants, birds or work. Some of their friends lived on farms, but even these seemed to have a curiosity value.

On my father's side, the world of farms was familiar. My Uncle John worked on a farm near Dunmore East and my father often spoke of doing farm-work in his boyhood. He told me of old-fashioned farm machinery and of how his hands were sometimes sore after a day of threshing.

For myself, the countryside had something of the familiarity with which my father treated it and something of the sightseeing value with which my mother's family regarded it. There were a number of farms in the countryside outside John's Park. The fields stretched as far as the roads on the edge of the estate and were natural places for children to explore. The fields near the top of the estate were part of the mental hospital grounds and sometimes I saw rows of bowed and silent patients from the hospital walking along the lanes after an afternoon spent working in potato-drills.

A ruined house in one of those fields was known as the Haunted House. Trying to instil fear into each other and to impress with how much we knew of it, we looked at it through hedges and spoke of the ghost of a German who was said to haunt it at night. A Luger pistol, we heard, had been found under its floorboards.

Getting chased by farmers was one of the dangers and attractions of the fields. Myself and other indifferent children waded through crops as if barley and wheat were as worthless as old cardboard. Furious farmers came running over ditches and gave chase.

Sometimes, this tormenting of the farmers became more serious. Animals were taunted and teased. Barns were entered for a dare and cows were chased across fields. A boy from the Main Road, out in the fields with his friends, was dared to pee on an electric fence. He opened his fly and peed away; the scream he emitted when the shock went through him could be heard back in the streets.

Another boy climbed up on a pregnant heifer and rode her around the field, beating her with a stick until the animal collapsed. The pressure and terror brought on her calf and she gave birth weeks before her time. I saw that dead, undeveloped calf lying in the grass the next day. Just over the ditch from it, children were playing in the streets and the battered wreck of a car lay near a gap. The dead calf was foetal and smooth; its eyes were no more than slits. It was a pale brown colour and lay with its legs hunched up and without a trace of hair on its hide. I watched as the farmer dug a hole and shovelled the calf into it. He spread quicklime over the clay after filling in the grave.

The boy was caught and taken to court where he faced a tough judge who was disgusted by what he had done. He stared at him and said: 'This was a despicable act. Why did you do such a thing?' The boy shrugged his shoulders and said: 'I thought it was a donkey, your honour.'

In some ways, it would have been no surprise if the boy really had been as stupid as he pretended to be. The natural world was a limited place as far as many of us were concerned. What little we saw of it could often be cruel.

A number of men in the estate kept greyhounds. A small number of these dogs were raced in coursing events in a field just twenty minutes away from our street. I went there one day to see what it was like. Hundreds of people, most of them men, stood around a field. When a greyhound was set after a hare, they roared. Skidding and turning, like a brown ball blown across the grass, the hare dodged the dog. The dog's mouth was open. It ran with a graceful rhythm while the hare drew closer to the fence. Some hares were caught and torn apart by the dogs. I could see the torn entrails of a hare lying in the grass. Money changed hands.

To give his dogs a taste for these events, or to 'blood' them as it was put, one greyhound owner trained his animals by bringing them to a field near Richardson's farm. He released a cat from a sack and then let the greyhounds bound across the grass after the cat until they caught it and tore it to pieces.

Most of those who owned greyhounds had no involvement with such escapades and kept their dogs only for the weekly races in Kilcohan when they chased a mechanical hare around a track on the perimeter of the soccer field. These races took place on Tuesday and Saturday nights and I could hear the roar of the crowd from our kitchen.

At evening, these men walked their greyhounds along the footpaths of our street, the dogs straining at the leash when some small Jack Russell pup yapped at them from the safety of a sitting-room window. Curved and lean and long-faced, the greyhounds mostly padded along with their owners behind them. They seemed ugly animals, but I was fascinated by the way they ran at incredible speed, yet seemed merely to pat the ground with their light paws.

Other dog-lovers kept animals as pets. A few used them for badger-baiting or hunting rabbits. At all hours of the night, one of these dogs would start barking in a back garden. It would whine and send up a loud ululation that was taken up by the dog next door until soon it seemed as if the night was taken over by a choir of terriers and mongrels. 'Shut up,' a voice would shout from a bedroom window. If the dog persisted, as it often did, the owner came down, went out into the yard, and gave the beast such a kick that it whined in agony and then shut up.

We never had a dog. We had a white cat. My brother Aidan won a prize in the Texaco children's art competition and Tessie took him to Dublin to receive his award. The presentation took place in the Gresham Hotel which was, according to Tessie, the poshest hotel in the country. I imagined chandeliers and glittering cutlery, and I felt jealous. When they came back, Tessie said it had hardly been worth her while getting all dolled-up since she had spent most of the time drinking tea and chewing biscuits with mothers and father in a hall while the children waited for their names to be called.

A few days after they came back from Dublin, Tessie gave us a white female kitten. It lay curled in a box next to the fire, settled on an old jumper. The mother-cat, which lived mainly under a chair in Tessie's house, had given birth to five others. No-one would take them, so Tessie drowned them in a huge saucepan of water outside the back door. I found their tiny screams unbearable. We kept the white one and had to think of a name: Snowy, Snowball, Fluff. We finally decided to call her Gresham to mark the occasion of our Aidan visiting a great hotel.

Some men kept pigeons out the back. In a few kitchens, a bright budgie twittered as it stared at itself in a mirror. Mice turned up now and then and once one scuttled along the floor under my father's feet. He threw a wooden breadboard after it, missing the mouse but breaking the breadboard in two. It was the most violent thing I ever saw him do. The breadboard had been part of a wedding-present and that angered him even more than the mouse.

The strangest creature ever seen in John's Park turned up in Jackie O'Regan's shop. Jackie was opening a wooden box of bananas on his counter one morning when he heard something stir in the straw in which the fruit was settled. He looked in through a slit, saw nothing only bananas and thought he must have been imagining things. He kept opening the box, prising out nails and finally forcing open the top.

The straw stirred again. He took the cigarette from his lips and looked in. There, looking up at him from the green-skinned bananas, he saw the beady eyes of a snake. He was too shocked to speak. When he had regained his composure, he started to shove people out of the shop, hurrying out the women waiting for potatoes and the children leaning over the counter with pennies.

'Get out, get out!' he shouted. 'There's a snake in the banana box.'

The shop was cleared in no time and the customers stood outside. Quickly, a large crowd gathered as news of the snake spread. With the shop to itself, the snake hissed its way along the counter.

'Motherajesus, it's a rattlesnake,' said a woman.

'It'll poison everything,' said another.

It was decided to send for Peery Power, who lived just a few houses away from the shop. A middle-aged, muscular man whose hair was cut in an American-style crew-cut, Peery was famous for his bravery and toughness. Tessie said that when bodies went missing in the river, Peery, who was a diver, was sent to get them out. His courage knew no limits. A snake would be nothing to him.

He strode up to the shop with the sleeves of his jumper rolled up. The women gathered around him. 'Jesus, Peery, you're wicked brave,' they said to him. He went into the shop with the swaggering confidence of a sheriff entering a saloon. He looked at the snake. The snake looked at him. He went over to it as if it was a relative with whom he was about to shake hands. He put out his hand. In seconds, he had the snake by the throat and held it in such a way that it was immobilised, stuck there in his grip with its eyes out on stalks and half the women of John's Park looking in at it. He held it like that until the guards arrived and took it away in a container. Peery was the hero of the day and found no shortage of free drink in the pub that night.

Other exotic animals came only with the circus. It arrived once a year and usually pitched tent on the Erin's Own hurling ground, close to the city centre and about fifteen minutes from John's Park. Gardens from a row of terraced houses backed onto the side of the pitch.

One afternoon, I saw a camel wander away from the circus and stop near the end of a back garden. It moved its huge jaws and started to chew chunks from a privet hedge. The irate householder stormed out of the kitchen and ran up the garden. Panting and gasping, he stood before the camel and waved his hands wildly in the air.

'Get out. Get away outta that,' he said to the camel.

The camel ignored him and kept munching.

'I'll fecking shoot you,' he said to the camel.

The camel chewed ever deeper into the trimmed privet. It ripped away branches until the man was left with the strength to do no more than whisper, pleading with the hairy brown beast to leave his hedge alone.

Minutes later, the camel wagged its hump like a cheeky hussy wagging her bum. Then, without a care, it strode back towards the circus tent, bits of privet clinging to its lips. The man was left alone with what remained of his privet. He looked orphaned and lost.

Besides the countryside, we came into contact with the natural world in the public park in town. It was called the People's Park and I preferred running around the bandstand or hiding behind a preserved cannon to studying its flowers and trees. I knew the names of very few trees and could name more television programmes than flowers. Like my father, I loathed anything to do with gardening.

I preferred the small things in nature to the big things. An elephant would have been of interest for a few minutes, but it was nothing compared to the fascination with which I watched thousands of ants scurrying around the cracks in the footpath outside the back door, or when I nudged a ladybird with a twig as it went still on the side of a blade of grass in the garden.

One of the nearby farms was owned by Paddy Spenser, with whom Des Gloster was friendly. Des was my closest friend in school. We had each known the death of a parent and this may have forged a bond between us. I often went with him to Paddy's farm. It was just a few minutes away from our houses and we got there by climbing over ditches and walking through the fields. I loved its smells — silage, hay, warm milk; and its sounds — the milking-machine, the heavy clop of cattle through the yard.

Paddy Spenser's family had long been associated with those few acres, but he told me he could see the day coming when the houses and the streets would spread even further than John's Park and eventually engulf the fields and ditches that he knew off by heart like a book.

Paddy was careful and meticulous in his work; he moved at his own pace and believed in not trying to do everything at once. 'Always keep a job until tomorrow,' he would say. Des was far more useful with his hands than I was and he would often help Paddy with small jobs around the farm. I lacked the ability and the confidence for such work. I was all thumbs.

My main pleasure came from being in the fields. One evening, I sat hunched with Des in the grass as Paddy helped a heifer give birth. The afterbirth lay in the grass. Midges pestered the heifer's eyes as it licked its calf. I was silent before the scene.

I was silent as well when I walked the fields on my own. Being alone was always special for me, whether in a room, in a cove in Dunmore East, or in one of Paddy's fields. I loved to sit on a rock in a place we called the Knock where now and again Paddy set fire to wild growths of gorse. Sitting there on my own, I could see across County Waterford to the Comeragh mountains and across the smoky city as well. I could hear a tractor droning in the distance and see a car pass a gate at the edge of the field below me near a house where a tramp lived in a shed. The voices of children were carried on the wind. Finally, I felt a deep, rich silence from which the rest of life would later seem an aberration.

As darkness fell, I headed back home to the streets and kept that silence inside me, sheltering it, as if to speak even one syllable would break its spell and shatter it forever.

If I sensed a hollow space after my mother's death, the space in which my father moved must have been more hollow still, but I was too young to comprehend it. When he decided to get married, he came home from the Merchant Navy and went to work in the new paper mills. There was a family story that he had run away to sea in his late teens. My grandmother was horrified, but my grandfather took a different attitude: 'Let Richie go,' he said. 'It'll make a man of him.'

When he was twenty, he joined the Irish Navy at Haulbowline in County Cork, enlisting in the first line reserve. It was mostly office work and it bored him. He looked out of the office window and saw, across a grey stretch of water, the tall cathedral in Cobh and the houses set around it as if they had tumbled higgledy-piggledy down the streets and hills of the town. On weekends, he went with his mates into Cobh, but since he had no interest in pubs or alcohol, he had a different social life from his friends. He went to the dancehall in Cobh or on walks, but his fixed, restrained upbringing had set its own standards and demands.

It was in a dancehall that he met my mother. The Fisherman's Hall in Dunmore East was a tiny community hall where bands came at weekends to play the songs of Glen Miller and Joe Loss before an audience of locals and visitors from the city. When my parents met in the early fifties, they were in their late twenties.

They started courting and when my father went back to sea they wrote to each other. He left the Irish Navy and joined the more adventurous and less-disciplined merchant service, travelling the world and noting ports-of-call in a small black-covered diary. He wrote brief accounts of the weather as well, remarking on the ferocity of waves around Cape Horn and the viciousness of sudden storms which drove him, he noted briefly, to a recitation of the rosary.

'The sea is marvellous, but water can hypnotise you,' he said to me. 'If you stand at the back of a ship and stare into the wake where the water's churning, you'll want to jump in eventually. It can be the same if you stare for long enough at a weir or a waterfall.'

My father seldom talked of the many places he had visited. It sometimes sounded as if he had never been anywhere but the inside of a ship. When abroad, he seldom ate at local restaurants, but kept to the ship's diet. Curries or pasta were not for him: stews and steak were safer and more like home. The house held few mementoes of his travels. A photograph showed him sitting cross-legged next to what looked like an Indian guru. An African fan, made from twisted reeds, was pinned to the sitting-room wall. A sailor's identity card, with photograph and fingerprints, lay in a bunch of papers.

'You can get Africa fever,' he said. 'You've been there once and you'll want to go there again. It gets a grip on you.' He could say the names of the thirty-two points of the compass as fast as a child counting to ten. And when he spoke of ships he had known, he referred to each one as 'she'. I imagined ships as women. When he discussed them, they seemed more like sisters than objects.

During the time of their courtship, my mother worked as a shop assistant in Dunnes Stores in Waterford. My father sent postcards to her there or to her home in Griffith Place. He called her Mo, just as Maureen Connolly, the famous tennis-player, was known as Little Mo. The postcards held brief conventional messages to Mo, a few words of slanted handwriting from some faraway port. The cards mostly showed ships or harbours.

When he finally came back to Waterford to settle down, my father left the sea behind him like an old coat, but the sea never really left him behind. Listening to the weather forecast remained an important part of his life and from him I learned the names of the coastal stations — Fastnet, Malin, Rockall, German Bight, Finistere — in much the same way as others learned the names of football teams. During a gale warning, the names came from the radio in a rhythm of their own. He listened to gale warnings with the interest of a man who expected the gale to come ripping through our kitchen at any moment.

After getting married, my parents lived briefly in a flat in Waterford but they eventually were given a corporation house. It must have seemed a time of good omens. It was the mid-fifties and factories were starting to open up. Emigrants came home to get jobs and, for the first time, they could make plans to settle down in Ireland. New housing estates went up to accommodate the new working-class families. The estates, with their reddish roofs and small gardens like ours, went up as cities expanded. Where my father had gone barefoot to school, his own children would at least wear shoes.

It was Seán Lemass, the Fianna Fáil Taoiseach, who opened the new factories and his picture was constantly in newspapers as he cut ribbons in industrial estates. He seemed to have a scissors stuck to his hand. Yet it was to Eamon de Valera that my father gave the greatest praise. When the bishop of Waterford died and his funeral was held in the cathedral, my father took me along and held me up to see de Valera, just as children of another age and place had been held up to see Queen Victoria. Tall and old, de Valera leaned on a soldier's arm and made his way through the high doors of the cathedral.

'Dev is the man,' my father said. It was de Valera's simple rural and nationalist vision that my father shared, but it was Lemass's pragmatism that he most admired. No matter how poor we might be, my father always believed it would be worse if Fianna Fáil was not in power. In this way, it seemed as if his world was a child born in the warm womb of Fianna Fáil and anyone who felt otherwise was an outsider.

The paper mills was one of the first factories to open in Waterford before the new industrial boom began in the sixties. It stood on the River Suir just a few miles along the Kilkenny side of the river. A tall stack marked it out in the distance and when Kilkenny played in the All-Ireland final, a black-and-amber flag flapped in the breeze at the top of the stack.

Like my father, most of those who went to work there were young. Like him as well, many came from rural backgrounds and this was their introduction to the industrial process. With the exception of a few packers, secretaries and canteen staff, the workers were male. The company was American-owned and its main products were large cardboard boxes, for everything from cornflakes to toilet rolls.

Every day, lorry-loads of waste paper came to the factory. Each lorry was weighed at the entrance and then, minus the load, it was weighed as it left. In this way, the weight of the waste paper was calculated and payment was made. Waste paper was also taken to the factory by ship. The ships anchored at a jetty and the paper was unloaded and brought to a large area behind the plant. The paper included bales of shredded pornography, stacks of remaindered books and unsold magazines. My father brought home many of the books for me. I was too young to understand them but, in some strange way, they struck a clear chord of appreciation.

My father read few books himself. Cowboy books were among those he liked, especially the novels of Zane Grey, but his favourite book, like his past, had to do with ships: *The Cruel Sea* by Nicholas Monserrat. All his books were stacked in one small set of varnished shelves my grandfather had made from herring-boxes. There were a few book club choices, my mother's large bulky copy of *Gone with the Wind*, and a number of books on the 1916 Rising and the subsequent years. I read these as I grew up: *Four Glorious Years* by Piaras Béaslaí, *Allegiance* by Robert Brennan, *My Fight for Irish Freedom* by Dan Breen.

To this selection I added the books he brought home. They included a small edition of *Twenty Years A-Growing* by Muiris Ó Súilleabháin, which I read when I was eleven and in my last year at primary school, and a collection of ancient Irish poems which had been written by monks in the margins of manuscripts.

I grew up thinking that the paper mills was full of such books, like a library. It was only when I went to work there myself in my late teens that I found out about the pornography. It lay in tightly bound stacks. Sometimes the men would rip into the stacks, trying to piece together the shredded strips that joined like a jigsaw to show naked women, whose pictures would then be pinned to the door of a locker where overalls and lunch-boxes were kept. Otherwise, the waste paper was all thrown into huge vats, where it was mixed into a pulp and eventually made into cardboard.

Huge rolls of paper also came to the factory. They were

lifted onto rollers and then spun through machines until they were joined together as cardboard. Once, a roll of paper slipped and rolled against one of the workers. It killed him. A black cross marked the wall close to the place where he died.

Some machines made corrugated paper; others folded boxes. Men stood on the side of long rollers and counted the boxes into piles as they came off the production line. Over the loud noise of the machines, men sang and whistled and cursed and shouted. They had their own vocabulary: 'showery,' meant scatter because the boss is coming; 'mullocking,' meant idling.

I never really understood my father's unskilled role in the factory. I found it hard to work out exactly what he did and I do not think he was too sure himself. He had gone to work each morning by the time I woke up, and when he came home in the evening he was wearing his factory clothes: an old jacket and trousers, and shoes on which factory dust had settled. He might have an old book in his pocket or a small stack of cardboard squares in his hand. These squares were for me. I took them into school where teachers distributed them for projects. Otherwise, the factory had no real shape for me, though its rhythms of payday and holiday and overtime decided the pattern of our lives.

Some other men in John's Park also worked in the paper mills. Others worked in the glass factory, the best job of all. More worked in the iron foundry or in Clover Meats, or in the bucket factory, or the chipboard factory, or as bus conductors and drivers. Most started work at eight each morning and many of those with cars gave lifts to those who did not own one.

My father was badly paid, as was everyone in the paper mills. We would certainly never have known a holiday if my grandparents had not lived in a cottage in Dunmore East. We had no fridge or washing-machine and we never had a car.

The quality of our lives deteriorated immediately when the workers in the paper mills went on strike for higher pay. My father went on picket-duty and attended union meetings at the ITGWU headquarters in Connolly Hall. The strike pay was minimal. Parcels of food came to the front door. The strike went on for five months and, when it was over, the workers had won a small pay increase. The benefits seemed minimal. There were more bills than usual after the strike but my father's pay, while a little higher than before, was very low indeed. There was still no money in the house on Thursdays.

Nonetheless, the paper mills lasted as the source of our sustenance. Its loud machines, bad conditions and swirling vats were a world away from the ships and harbours where my father had once worked. For my mother, the world of the city and its streets was a natural stomping-ground. It was different with my father. Housing estates, chimney stacks and cardboard boxes were a long way from the sea, which he missed as if it was a girlfriend he had once known intimately but whose advances he had been forced by circumstances to reject.

Tessie often took us to Lady Lane, a street in the centre of town with buildings that I feared but a name that I liked. Halfway along the street, a weathered stone head was fixed to a wall near the Franciscan Friary. Carved and expressionless, it stared into the street like a death-mask. I knew nothing about it, but imagined it as the head of a woman who had been turned to stone after falling from the top of a tower.

'What are you looking at that old thing for?' Tessie asked. 'Come on, or we'll be late for the dispensary.'

She took us to the dispensary in Peter Street, near Lady

Lane, when we were sick. We had a medical card and so were entitled to free medical services. Doctors came to the house if one of us was sick enough, but if we were only mildly ill, Tessie took us to the dispensary.

The place frightened me. It lay at the end of a narrow path which began under a stone arch near the road. Its bare wooden floors were slippery on wet days and water dripped from umbrellas resting inside the door. Women sat on long pews, their shopping-bags beside them. We sat near them and waited our turn.

The doctor worked in a room near the pews. Most of the doctors in the dispensary were jovial but some who worked there for a few weeks, when the others were on holiday, could be sharp-tongued and impatient. One young doctor looked at patients through glasses which lay at the tip of his nose. If he was in a bad mood, he barked out questions, and made lame jokes if the mood was right. He performed a trick with his fingers, making me think that the top of his thumb was coming away from his hand. I wasn't too sure about it and only half-laughed.

'Let's put you up here,' he said. He sat me on the side of a table. 'Take off your shirt.' He pressed the stethoscope against my bare chest. Its coldness caught me by surprise, but to flinch would have been cowardly. The room was heated by a paraffin burner which gave off a heavy smell of oil which added to the oppressive and stuffy atmosphere. Rain beat against the high windows that framed a grey sky.

He pinched my skin. 'There's not much of you in it,' he said. He pressed what looked like a wide lollipop stick against my tongue. 'Say aaahh.'

'Aaaaaahh.' I hated the feel of the dry stick against my tongue. It was one of those things, like the sound of chalk scraping against the blackboard, or the thought of ice against my spine, that made me cringe and shiver. 'Louder,' he said and pressed my tongue down even further. 'Aaaaaaaahh,' I groaned. I thought I was going to vomit.

He pressed his fingers beneath my eyes and drew down the lower lids. 'White as ghosts,' he said. 'You're anaemic. He's anaemic,' he said to Tessie. 'He needs plenty of iron. Give him a feed of liver and cabbage. Bottles of milk. Too much indoors. Give him this twice a day.'

'Yes, doctor,' said Tessie. He wrote a prescription on a white sheet of paper. A shining curved scales in which babies were weighed was set on a shelf behind him. Tessie's voice was low. She looked on doctors with great reverence. Like priests and the rent-man, they were part of a higher world in which her role was one of subservience.

'There's one more thing, doctor,' she said.

'Give him that now and he'll be right in a few weeks. Liver and cabbage.'

'There's one more thing, doctor,' she repeated.

'What?' he said. 'I've half the town waiting outside. What is it?'

Tessie's face went red and her shoulders became hunched. 'Bandages for my leg, doctor. I'm out of them. For my varicose veins.'

'Your leg? What's wrong with your leg? You're supposed to get those bandages yourself. The appointment was made only for the young fellow. Are you on the same medical card?'

'No, doctor. I have my own card here.' She took the card from her shopping-bag and handed it to him. Its creases were brown and cracked. He looked at it briefly.

'Do you know how many people are outside?' he asked. 'And you want bandages. You could get them in a chemist shop for a few pence.' He tapped his pen on the table in an impatient staccato.

'The usual doctor was here before and he told me I could get them on the medical card,' Tessie said. I thought she was going to cry.

The doctor sighed. 'Alright. But this is the last time you're getting them. There's nothing wrong with your leg that plenty of walking wouldn't cure and there's any amount of people who need bandages more urgently than you do.'

He wrote another prescription for the bandages and gave it to her. 'Thank you, doctor,' she said. 'I won't trouble you again.' She picked up the shopping-bag from the floor, took me by the hand and led me from the room. As we walked back to the room of crowded pews, an old woman rose and passed us. 'What kind of humour is he in?' she asked Tessie in a whisper.

'Like a fecking dog,' Tessie said.

The woman put her eyes to Heaven and blessed herself. 'Jesus, Mary and Joseph,' she said and walked on.

'That fella's a dog,' Tessie said. 'A proper dog.' We sat down in another group of pews set along a wall. This was the queue for prescriptions. It was as long as the queue for the doctor but it moved faster. Tessie lit a cigarette as we waited, sliding along the smooth seat as a space became vacant. Men whom I had seen around the streets waited in front of us. I had watched them drinking from bottles outside the hostel near the dispensary. One of them had a bottle in his pocket. Its top was sealed with a rag into which a cork was pressed.

When it came to her turn, Tessie rose and walked to a hatch set in a wall. A man with a round, red face opened the hatch and took the prescriptions from her. He closed the hatch again and I could hear a lock click shut. After a few minutes, the hatch opened and the man handed a bottle and a package to Tessie.

'One spoonful twice a day and bring back the bottle if you want more,' he said in a streaming sentence. 'Next,' he called.

Tessie thanked him, put the medicine and bandages in her bag and we left. The queue moved up.

After the stuffy air of the dispensary, the street outside was fresh and clear despite the rain. Ivy grew around the edge of the door. A woman passed us. 'He's like a dog in a kennel in there,' Tessie said.

'Some of those young ones are never any other way,' replied the woman.

We walked along Lady Lane in the rain. Tessie stopped near a high Georgian house. This was the Legion of Mary hostel where her friend, Maudie Cleary, worked. A woman stood outside with some bags on the footpath beside her. A dirty scarf was tied around her head. Her long grey coat stretched down to her ankles. She looked up at the windows of the hostel and let out a long wail. The thought of passing her was too much to take.

'Come on,' said Tessie. 'She's half cracked. Don't mind her. She stays in the hostel, but they won't let her in when she gets like that.'

We waited in the hallway of the hostel for Tessie's friend to arrive. Women passed in and out. Many seemed poor or disturbed. One or two looked at me and smiled. A huge statue of Our Lady was fixed to the wall. I could hear a woman singing somewhere up the stairs.

Her friend came down the stairs and left the hostel with us. Tessie often spoke about the Legion of Mary and, when I was ten, persuaded me to join a branch which met in the school in John's Park. The meetings lasted for hours and were full of strange words like *praesidium* and *legionis*, while we were supposed to refer to each other as 'Brother'. Our work in the Legion consisted mostly of visiting old people in the Mathew Shea hostel in Poleberry. I hated going there, talking to old women who sat in rooms full of old newspapers and faded photographs.

I gave up the Legion of Mary one night after a meeting in John's Park. The meetings made me tense as I sat through interminable prayers and exaggerated accounts of work we had done. A cloth bag was passed around at the end of each meeting and we were supposed to place money in it. This bag was known as the Secret Bag because no-one was to know how much anyone else had put in it. It struck me suddenly that by the same token I could take money out of it and no-one would know anything about that either. Just before it began the round, I burst into nervous, uncontrollable laughter as often happened when I was tense. My stomach hurt with pain as I tried to stop. The tension of acting like a saint for an hour was too much. I keeled over with laughter. The chairman of the meeting stared at me and other boys shuffled in their seats.

'When Brother Dunne is finished, we'll pass around the Secret Bag,' he announced. I laughed even louder, pressing my teeth together to try to stop, but my mouth hurt with the effort. I left the meeting and never went back.

Tessie's friend never asked me why I had stopped going. When I saw her in the hostel, I felt nervous that she might ask this time but she said nothing. We walked away from Lady Lane and went around by the Protestant cathedral. There was a wide step there where I was told a murder had once been committed. I had heard that at night ghostly blood seeped from the stone and ran down the steps.

This was the oldest part of Waterford. Its narrow streets led to the quays. Georgian houses aged into a slow decay of flats and apartments where milk bottles lay next to plastic plants in front of net curtains. Walking through these streets on Sunday afternoons, I thought of it as a deserted area where no-one walked except patients from the mental hospital wandering through town, or winos, who sat on footpaths waiting for the hostel to open.

If we were in this part of town on holy days, when we were off school and obliged to attend mass, Tessie sometimes took us into the Friary. It was a dark and gloomy church. Just like the streets, every church had an atmosphere of its own. The Friary was very popular with old people. The Franciscans had a reputation for extreme holiness and I was in awe of them in winter when I saw them walk through the streets with sandals on their red, bare feet. One of them was said to carry a piece of the true cross. His nickname was Splinter.

Tessie also took us to the Friary on the feast of Saint Blaise. Then, we queued before the altar and a priest took two candles and crossed them against our throats. The name Blaise and the use of candles unnerved me, as if I was about to be engulfed by blazing fire. This ceremony was meant to keep our throats free of infections and disease for a year. In the same way, Tessie hung rags on the clothesline the night before Saint Bridget's Day. She kept the rags and believed they had special powers to ease sickness.

Narrow streets surrounded many of the inner-city churches. My favourite was a tiny street which led off George's Street to Saint Patrick's Church, the oldest in the city. It was seconds away from the car-filled streets, but its atmosphere was one of centuries-old silence and calm. I sat and watched candles flicker in rows and heard a tinkle when a penny was slipped through a slit in the collection box near the door. A huge, life-like crucifix hung on the wall in the narrow lane outside. This was the only thing I disliked about the church. The blood on the crucifix was too realistic and there was too much of it. It was frightening and ugly.

The inner-city streets had their particular inhabitants. Near the clock-tower on the quays, a stout man wearing a number of coats threw bread to pigeons. He shuffled along as the pigeons pecked at the ground around him. I was fascinated by people like him. They seemed to inhabit a strange world of their own, separate from everyone but nonetheless part of everyone's life. Another was a small man who stood next to a suitcase of cheap toys near a car park. He seemed to have a smile fixed to his face, a simple, child's smile that grew whenever he sold a water pistol or a plastic windmill that spun in the breeze. The woman I saw near the hostel was another such person and she frequently wailed her way through the streets with her collection of bags from which old clothes and papers protruded. Every so often, she would stop and give a loud lecture to the skies, her grey hair straggling around her face.

Tessie's friend left us near the City Hall. 'We'd better hurry on,' Tessie said, 'or we'll miss the bus.' We stood at the bus stop near the Car Stand. Boxes of expensive chocolates were arranged in the window of Jackie O'Regan's shop behind us. He owned a shop in John's Park as well, but this shop had classier things for sale. Music blared from Sinnott's record shop across the road. I got the smell of chips coming from Delicato's chip-shop.

A thin man with no teeth and a blue overcoat fell against Tessie. I had seen him often on the bus and he was always drunk. He put a cigarette into his mouth and asked Tessie for a light. His voice was slurred. The cigarette was upside-down.

'I have no light,' she said. We edged away from him. He straightened the cigarette and asked again. The bus came around the corner and stopped. I could see the creases in his mouth where his lips seemed sucked in by his gums. His dark hair was Brylcreemed and tossed. He swung around the bus-stop like an ape in a nature programme.

'That fella's a right eejit,' Tessie said. The bus conductor, who knew him, helped him onto the bus and I was worried that he would try and sit next to me. He talked loudly and incomprehensibly, shouting and singing and spilling coins on the floor as he looked for the fare. After a few stops, he got off the bus.

'Good riddance to bad rubbish,' said a man.

'The poor devil can't help it I suppose,' said Tessie, softening. 'I knew him when he was only a young fella.'

This was one of her common themes. She frequently talked of people she had known in 'her heyday,' and of how they had changed for the worst. It was as if her youth had been a time of dances and songs and promises and excitement until time shifted and replaced her youth with a world of narrow streets, broken people and dark, poky houses where cats crawled.

It was still raining when we got off the bus in John's Park. Teenagers stood smoking outside a shop near the bus-stop. Rain swept across the fields which faced the row of houses where the bus stopped. Across those fields lay places we sometimes explored, like Major Doheny's where it was rumoured a boy in our school had seen a naked girl riding a white horse around a lake. We cut bamboos there and took them home to use for making a high jump in the back garden.

Another set of fields, not far from Kilcohan Park, was known as Richardson's. There, acres of daffodils were cultivated. If I stood on top of a wall in spring, I could see them blooming, a gust swirling through them so that they all leaned in the one direction as if straining to hear something.

Not far from Richardson's, a road ran parallel with the street on which the bus had now stopped. This was a back road to Tramore and I suddenly remembered how I had often been taken on that road for walks by my mother, stopping near a gate-lodge to buy home-made butter. One day she took us into a field over a low wall near a narrow country lane. My brother and I played with her in the grass. Later, she sat and twirled her wedding-ring around her finger.

Something happened — one of us about to fall, a sandwich crumbling — and the wedding-ring slipped from her finger. We looked for hours through the grass. The ring was never found. This happened a month before she died.

Years later, as I looked across the fields from the bus-stop, I thought of the wedding-ring. Whenever I was on that road, I had gone into that field and searched in the grass for the ring. Even with the passing years, I thought I might still find it. Sometimes at night I imagined it lying there, glowing in the dark grass with a radiance that faded when morning dawned.

'Hurry on now or we'll get drenched,' Tessie said. We were home in a few minutes. 'Dry your hair,' she said and gave me a towel. I sat by the fire. She took down the iron and some clothes. She turned on the wireless and I heard a man read an episode from the story of Jane Eyre. He read of the mad Mrs Rochester and Grace Poole, the servant in the attic, and of the great fire in which the madwoman perished. I went back over the dark, wet day with its streets, its hostel, and its long wait at the dispensary. And I thought as well of the countryside near Kilcohan, and of the rain falling on my mother's wedding-ring buried in a field.

Like my father, many others in John's Park had arrived there from backgrounds different to the world in which they now lived. Some had come from the city or small towns, but many came from the Waterford and Kilkenny countryside and from coastal villages. Now they were all part of a working-class community. In this way, John's Park became a melting-pot, but some of those who lived there upheld an order which showed itself in small ways that might remain invisible to an outsider.

Our parents mostly had grown up in an impoverished Ireland. Now, as people stayed at home and factories seemed to be opening everywhere, there was a desire to get on in life. It was no longer the case that children would leave school, like my father, at the age of thirteen; neither would they walk barefoot through the streets and lanes with nothing before them only the boat to England or America.

Above us, there was the middle-class. They lived in other parts of Waterford like Grange Park and Newtown. Their streets had mature trees and their houses had large windows. Above them, in some realm that had as much meaning for me as a fairy castle, lived others with whom we never came into contact. These included filmstars and people like the Aga Khan or the McGrath family, who made a lot of money from an involvement in the Irish Sweepstakes and in Waterford Glass. They were names in a newspaper and touched our lives only in freakish, transient ways such as when Jacqueline Kennedy came on holidays to a house near Woodstown Strand, or Stanley Kubrick made a film in County Waterford which featured many people from John's Park as extras.

One day, Kubrick offered five pounds extra to anyone who brought a dog onto the set of *Barry Lyndon* the next morning. A man told me of how he had gone around John's Park in a van at dawn, gathering all the stray dogs he could find.

I saw the social order reflected in a way that was related to the amount of money my father brought into the house. He was paid on Friday and there was usually no money left by the following Wednesday at the latest. Thursday was a poor day and by tea-time there was little to eat besides the sliced pan which the breadman left on the windowsill. The breadman, who worked for the Gold Crust bakery, was paid on Saturday for the bread he left every day. It was the same with the milk and so we were never without these two staple foods. We sometimes bought food on credit in Doyle's shop. 'Tell him to put it on the book,' my father would say.

Friday was pay-day for most of the families around us. Since days of the week have a character of their own, Thursdays generally had a feeling of want, while Friday held an air of plenitude and surprise. The two local shops sold cheap meat on Thursdays, their windows boasting stacks of pigs' tails and offal. There were large bones we called chucks and thin bones we called handles, which were used to make stews. On Thursdays in summer, when many of the doors along our road were open, I could get the smell of these stews filling the street, some of them carrying the faint tang of boiled kidney.

Those families whose men worked in the glass factory were by far the best off. The wages in the glass factory were legendary and money was especially plentiful for these families at holiday-time when the workers were paid hefty bonuses. They and their families were among the first to go on foreign holidays. They went to resorts in Spain, where many of them booked into the same hotels. Up to then, people went mostly to Tramore, or to England to see relatives, or to Butlin's holiday camp at Mosney in County Meath. My parents went to Mosney on their honeymoon and I have a photograph of my mother there, sitting in front of a fountain in a cardigan and dress, the sleeves of the cardigan rolled up.

From one house to the next, small signs indicated social and local status. Some families seemed especially interested in status while others, because they felt secure or indifferent, or had simply despaired, had no interest in it at all. When the estate was finished, all the houses looked the same but small changes were made with time. All the front doors had letterboxes and metal knockers. In time, some families got doorbells and this, to me, seemed a sign of social mobility. Even within the range of doorbells, there was a kind of pecking order: older, broken or cheap bells gave a deep, growling noise when pressed. Sometimes it was necessary to press the button very hard to get any sound at all. In the same way, new, with-it doorbells worked the minute you pressed them and gave a clear, deliberate ring. One or two gave off loud ornate chimes similar to those heard at the entrances to big houses in American television series.

The metal knocker fell from some letterboxes and was not replaced. Then you had to knock by pressing in the metal flap of the letter-box a few times. Some of these metal flaps were stiff; others seemed as loose as gold-leaf paper and they rattled limply in the wind.

The number of each house was screwed into the front door above the letterbox. On some doors, these original numbers had been taken off and replaced by wooden or cheap plastic digits. A lamp was added to some porches. A few windows had net curtains; others had Venetian blinds or, like ours, plain curtains. Neither the houses nor the streets had official names. We called the streets by simple names: the Main Road, the Square, the Back Road. An older street outside John's Park was called Pearse Park while the road past the Ursuline Convent was known as the Ursuline Road. Later, an effort was made to introduce official names. One road was then called Cherry Blossom Avenue, but that never really caught on.

At the start, all the gardens looked the same but, in time, took on a personality of their own. Some of the front gardens were well-tended and soon sprouted flowers and hedges. When we played in the street, we ran in and out of the gardens as if they made up one big field and arguments sometimes occurred with the owners when children fell against young hedges or crouched in trimmed privet during games. We played on the road as well, and the footpaths became sites for mock shops made from upturned cardboard boxes on which were displayed a range of comics and broken toys that could be purchased for bottle-tops (we called them 'tee-tees') gathered in bags around the back of the pub near the Main Road.

Some gardens were walled off eventually, another small sign

of social improvement. Gardens like ours had neither wall nor developed hedge because my father had no interest in gardening and even less in walls. The back garden was the same. The clothesline was its only obvious feature. In winter, the grass grew to resemble a low jungle. In summer, we trampled the grass down with our games.

I preferred a rough, untended garden. At the start of summer, the grass was still high enough to hide in and I lay in it with comics, the pages growing warm in the sun. In the tall grass, I could see butterflies, grasshoppers or ladybirds and hear birds singing, though I never knew their names. There was a hedge at the end of the garden and I worked out a way of sitting comfortably in it, perched there and cut off from the world like Robinson Crusoe.

From the window of my father's bedroom, I could see across to the kitchens and back bedrooms of the houses behind us. I could also see the back gardens and the make-up of each told a lot about its owners. One had rough kennels for dogs. Another was neatly filled with vegetables and its sides were blocked with wood of all shapes and sizes, or with sheets of corrugated metal that kept dogs from trampling and chasing through the rows of cabbages and potatoes. Another garden might have a greenhouse, made from stretched plastic set on poles and placed against the back of a coalshed. In another lay the frame of an old bicycle rusted among stacks of empty Guinness bottles. Large holes pocked the surface where children played with shovels, sticking toy soldiers in heaps of clay.

Every house had a radio. My father called it the wireless. It was a heavy brown-boxed affair with the names of different countries and places, including Athlone and Hilversum, written on the dial. When he turned it on, a light glowed in front of the name of whatever station it was tuned to. By turning the dial, I could move across the world with the small, glowing light, searching through the crackle and static for a familiar voice or hearing voices speak in many languages.

In the afternoons, the sound of sponsored programmes on Radio Éireann came from the kitchens: the Glen Abbey Show, the Nescafé Programme, the Walton's Programme on Saturdays, which told us that if we were going to sing a song, then we should sing an Irish song. My father was always cooking a fry when the Walton's Programme came on, and the sizzling of rashers made a background against which the old-fashioned songs were heard: 'The Stone Outside Dan Murphy's Door', 'The West's Awake'.

When I was eight, I saw television for the first time in a neighbour's house. There were very few television sets in John's Park. The only models were black-and-white, though I had heard that in America it was possible to get a television that showed colour pictures. The first programme I saw was a cowboy series starring the Cisco Kid. We crowded into a sitting-room, where it seemed half the children in John's Park were camped, and watched the flickering black-and-white images.

Gradually, more and more families got televisions and in time — though it seemed a long time — we got one too. In a few homes, a transparent plastic sheet was placed over the television and this gave a kind of colour effect that worked best with outdoor scenes since the plastic held only a few colours: blue (for the sky in the top part of the screen) and green (for the grass in the lower part) were predominant.

All the televisions were large and bulky and the only channel was an Irish one. In some houses, the weekly television guide was bought at weekends but most relied on the daily papers for listings. Television characters took over our games and our talk. There was the Fugitive, a man named Richard Kimble who, every week, tried to dodge the policemen who wanted him for a crime he had not committed. He was looking for a one-armed man, who entered our mythology in much the same way as Cuchulainn or Oisin, or any of the other heroes we were told about at school. Tales of Fionn and the Fianna were all very well, but the army that interested me most was the haphazard and wayward cavalry regiment in a television series called 'F-Troop'.

By the time every house had a television, colour television had arrived in Ireland and this became the next thing to get. Cars were also becoming more prominent: the greatest status symbols of all. Anglias, Minis and Morris Minors were in the majority. The narrow roads in John's Park made it difficult to park, so a few people poured concrete over the grass in their front garden and turned it into a driveway, fronted by metal gates with spiralling bars or ornate, twisted loops curled like the tails of sea horses.

None of the houses had a telephone, an item that seemed as out of reach as any of the other trappings of wealth we saw in television programmes. The only telephone in the estate was a public call-box situated in the Square. It was often vandalised, its windows broken, its coin-box torn out and its silent receiver dangling limply from ripped-out wire.

Most houses had linoleum covering the floors, but carpets replaced it as time went on. We had lino on all the floors and this made them cold to walk across in the mornings or during the night. The edges faded away in time and if I pulled back the corners on the top of the stairs, I could see a few old yellowing sheets of newspaper underneath — *The Irish Press* from the late fifties, or pages from the *Waterford News and Star*.

Carpets were bought mostly in town. Sometimes, as in our house, they were bought from travellers who called to the door. My father haggled over the cost; he was always very pleased when he brought the price down. It was the countryman in him: 'You have to be able to handle them fellows,' he said. 'They'll always bring the price down if you haggle with them.' He whistled in satisfaction.

Others called weekly to the door as well. There was Mr Roche from the Torch Club, a local pools; Mr Mulhall called for insurance money; Jimmy Spenser, the milkman, came for his money on Saturday morning and Billy the breadman came on Saturday afternoon; Pat Kelly called for the Gael Linn pools; someone from the Parish Committee collected for the new church; the Development Association representative for a new hall. Agents from shops in town also called, each with a small book into which was ticked the amount my father paid every week towards clothes, shoes or furniture.

The rent-man came on Tuesday morning and he was by far the most important person to pay. If the rent went unpaid for more than two weeks, a kind of panic set in and a lot of things had to be done without to make up the amount. On weeks when the rent had been forgotten or was not to hand, Tessie made sure she was out when Mr Cunningham, the rent-man, came knocking. If we were on holidays from school when he knocked in those circumstances, Tessie made us stand still in the kitchen and not say a word until the knocking was over and he had gone away. I felt that my thumping heart was the loudest thing on earth as I waited for him to leave.

Our account in Doyle's shop had to be paid up frequently. Once a week, a box of groceries was delivered to the front door. The box held only basics and these were made to last for as long as possible. There were very few luxuries, a weekly bag of biscuits being the most obvious. Sweets and chocolate were rarities. One of my friends, Ronan Sheehy, bought a bar of Caramilk chocolate every day on the way to school. To me, he seemed impossibly rich. I wasn't envious, but I made sure that I always got a square of his chocolate.

Lunch was what you ate during the school-break in the morning. Dinner was what you had when you went home after the morning's school. In the evening, you had your tea.

At night, you had a snack for supper. From television, and especially from English-made programmes, I learned that other people had lunch while we had dinner. It was cooked by a woman called Mummy, while the women in our estate were called Mammy. To call your mother Mummy in John's Park would have been a sign of severe affectation.

While the school that I and other boys attended was in the heart of the estate, the girls went to school in the Ursuline Convent just outside John's Park. The convent had a reputation for snobbery. Up to then, it had been a boarding school catering for the daughters of prosperous Catholic middle-class families. Girls from well-off parts of Waterford went there as day-pupils and so, when the girls of John's Park were taken in as pupils, the school became an uneasy mixture of types. It was believed locally that the nuns, who had been used to prim, nicely mannered, well-spoken girls up to then, had less time for the girls from John's Park. My Aunt Bessie believed this and eventually asked my father to take Breda out of the Ursuline Convent. She transferred to the Presentation Convent where my mother had gone to school. It was farther away but that wasn't the point.

Many of the girls in the Ursuline, as we called their school, came from Grange Park and Newtown. I sometimes went for walks through these areas. They seemed to exude wealth. Houses were semi- or fully detached and in the gardens I saw trees and beds of well-tended flowers set among lawns. Through windows, I could see rooms larger than any in John's Park. Cars were parked in large driveways and the children who played in the gardens seemed better-dressed than any I knew. Their skin was clear and healthy and none had that pasty-faced look that marked some of the children in John's Park. They also had a kind of confidence that was foreign to me. When I went to Sister Augustine in the convent for singing lessons, I met girls from these places and felt uncertain beside their easy and assured air of knowing their place in the world.

Although we were just fifteen minutes or so away from these children, we never mixed with them. They might as well have been in Tasmania. We kept to our own streets and our own kind, our world defined by our houses, our accents, our gardens, our clothes and even our shoes. From head to toe, we were children of Saint John's Park and, while within the streets and between the houses a kind of pecking order sometimes prevailed, we were all still on the same rung of the ladder, fixed firmly, it seemed, in our own place.

One morning in 1966, when I was nine, Tessie sat at the kitchen table and placed her shopping-bag before her. 'I have something special for you here,' she declared.

She rummaged and took out a paper bag of soft pears blotched with brown. I looked at them with disgust. 'Where the feck is it gone?' she said. Fixing a cigarette between her lips, she plunged her hand deeper into the shopping-bag and took out balls of wool wrapped in a knitting pattern. 'Jesus, Mary and holy Saint Joseph. Am I after losing it or what?'.

Other things came out of the bag and soon the table was covered with the odds and ends she accumulated as she went from shop to shop and bus-stop to bus-stop. I disliked her sense of chaos. I liked the things around me to be in their place and was always arranging my toys and books in an orderly way. Likewise, I went through the rows of ornaments on the shelf in the kitchen above the cupboard in which food was kept. Those ornaments included china dolls and a set of porcelain houses with roofs that came away. Everything was stuffed into those houses, from bits of twine to safety-pins, from old bus-tickets to rent receipts. Every few months, I sorted the whole lot out, poring with fascinated care over the stray, mundane objects that made up the everyday life of our home.

Eventually, Tessie's hand fixed on something and she exhaled a puff of cigarette smoke. 'I found it,' she said. 'I thought I was after losing it. It cost me a fortune. If someone robbed it on me, they'd swing for it.'

She placed a small package before me. It was wrapped in a brown paper bag twisted tightly at the top. I opened the bag and found a white octagonal plastic box of the sort that communion medals came in.

'Open it. We'll say Up The Republic just this once. My poor father would turn in his grave if he saw me buying this.' I prised open the lid and saw a silver coin resting on a bed of cotton wool. I knew immediately what it was: a special ten-shilling piece issued to mark the fiftieth anniversary of the 1916 Rising. One side of the coin showed a profile of Patrick Pearse, one of the leaders of the insurrection, while the other showed the figure of Cuchulainn. 'He looks plastered drunk if you ask me,' Tessie said, holding Cuchulainn up to the light. 'There's hardly a stitch on him. Up the rebels how are you. It'll be worth millions in years to come. You'll remember me by it.'

Ten shillings was an enormous amount of money and I thought of many things I could have bought with it in O'Regan's shop. A number of my classmates had been given these coins, but the word went around that you could not actually spend them. They weren't real money, like a ten-shilling note. This gift from Tessie was a useless coin.

Knowing her pro-British sympathies, I realised that a part of her must have softened momentarily. She would not have shared the aims of the Easter Rising. There were times when she wished Ireland was still ruled by Britain, which was a land of lucrative pensions, plentiful employment, large knickers and Vera Lynn.

The main purpose of the 1916 coin, we were told in school, was to mark a great event. *Éirí Amach na Cásca* the Brothers called it — Gaelic for the Easter Rising. A framed copy of the 1916 Proclamation was hanging on every classroom wall in the school. I knew all the names and faces, from old Tom Clarke, who had been a Fenian and had run a tobacco shop, through to Joseph Mary Plunkett, a pale poet whose poem 'I See His Blood upon the Rose,' was in one of my schoolbooks, and James Connolly, the socialist who had been executed while sitting injured in a chair.

A pageant was held in the school to mark the fiftieth anniversary of the Rising. The course of Irish history, from the battle of Clontarf to 1916, was enacted over the space of a few hours in a playing-field behind the school. We charged and fought in battle after battle, blithely acting out the battle of Clontarf with wooden swords and cardboard helmets. Through the school railings, I could see mothers holding up babies to look at us. At a special concert held in the playground, I sang 'Boolavogue', a song that told of the 1798 Rebellion in County Wexford.

Easter Week had always been a week with a dark mood of its own. It was a time of accumulating despair that seemed reflected in the weather. The flowers were taken from altars in churches, and statues were covered in purple as a collective gloom descended. Tessie took us to kiss the cross on Good Friday. We walked under skies that seemed always grey and, when we got to the church, queued in the aisle. When my lips touched the cold figure of Christ on the crucifix, I sensed the day darken with grief.

On Easter Saturday night, my father took me to the Easter

vigil. The lights of the church went out and the congregation stood in darkness. I moved closer to the smell of my father's overcoat until the Easter candle was lit, its glow taken up by other candles until the lights of the church were turned on again.

The power of the Easter Rising was now added to these symbols. Easter in 1966 became a time of dual resurrection: Christ's and Ireland's. For the first, the enemy was the Romans; for the second, it was the British. I learned in school of how crowds had gone to the races at Fairyhouse in 1916 while the rebels took over the GPO and other strategic points in Dublin. Facts flared in my head: a boat had taken guns to the Kerry coast but had been intercepted; the professorial Eoin MacNeill had tried to stop the rebellion; crowds looted shops as the rebels held out for a week against the British Army.

'It would be a shame to spend it,' my father said when he saw the special coin. This seemed a strange attitude towards money. I put the coin back in its box. Every so often I took it out, my mental cash register going berserk as I thought of its value growing with each day. I wondered why Patrick Pearse was always seen in profile, never from the front.

The 1916 Rising, which led to the eventual victory of the republicans, seemed to dominate events for a year. The same faces of the 1916 leaders who looked out from classroom walls also looked out from special commemorative stamps which, one by one, I collected and placed in a stamp-album. At Easter, a series called 'Insurrection' ran on television every night. The parts of Dublin where the Rising was centred became familiar place-names that featured in our games around the street: Mount Street Bridge; the GPO; Bolands Mills where de Valera, aged thirty-four, led the rebels. On a school trip to Dublin, I saw the pillars of the GPO pocked with what I took to be bullet-marks, and walked in the yard in

Kilmainham Jail where the leaders of the Rising had been shot. At Arbour Hill, I saw their graves.

Many people associated with that period were still alive. Among them was a friend of my grandmother's, an old woman called Molly McGrath, who lived in Poleberry, fifteen minutes from John's Park. I was often taken to visit her in her cramped, dark house. Surrounded by old furniture and fabrics, I sat staring at a photograph on the living-room wall. This showed Molly's brother, Michael, who had been shot dead by the British during an ambush at Pickardstown near Tramore during the Troubles.

Like my grandfather, Molly was a living link with the period of the Rising and its aftermath and I thought of her whenever I went to Tramore. I peered from the bus to catch a sight of the shrine at Pickardstown where commemorations were held every year. I was interested in the place also because, in more recent times, a man called Seán Hunt had been murdered in a chalet up the road from the shrine. The road past the Pickardstown grotto was a quiet country place. It was hard to imagine the noise of bullets and armoured cars against the leafy ditches that overlooked a shimmering view of the sea.

My father took me to many of the ceremonies and parades that marked the Rising celebrations. Old IRA men marched behind brass bands, their medals shining on heavy lapels as they saluted when the Last Post was played. I found it difficult to see them as young revolutionaries similar to those depicted in my school history books, where drawings showed keen faces lit by the glow of the burning GPO as Connolly urged them on from a stretcher.

I asked Tessie to get me a scrapbook in Woolworths and pasted newspaper cuttings that dealt with the Rising into its pages. I cut out photographs and recollections and eventually knew so much about it that I had no difficulty in mentally recreating its main events.

Despite the intensity with which the Rising was remembered, it was mainly a thing of the past. The distance became broken and more confused two years after the celebrations, when trouble broke out in the North. In 1968, I knew very little about the North, except that it was a place which came about after the Treaty. From songs and history books, I knew the names of nationalist rebels who came from there: Roddy McCorley, Henry Joy McCracken. From my grandfather, I had heard of the IRA's border campaign and one of the songs I learned was called 'Seán South of Garryowen', a ballad sung in memory of a Limerick IRA man who had been killed in an attack on Brookeborough RIC Barracks in the North.

I saw policemen on television attack a crowd of protesting civil rights campaigners. A policeman whacked a man with a baton and the man held his hand to his head, from which tributaries of blood poured. The trouble grew and became a focus of intense interest in our house as events spun and spiralled with an energy that made the street outside our sitting-room window seem mundane. The British Army moved into the North. The IRA came into action. Streets were set on fire. The fierce figure of Ian Paisley dominated the television screen. The Taoiseach, Jack Lynch, who appeared to be a timid, pipe-smoking man in comparison, made serious speeches which seemed calm when measured against the pace of events. People, incidents and events blurred and blended into one another as successive prime ministers of Northern Ireland presided over a collapse into chaos. I was in my first year in secondary school and found myself drawn into the emotions of the televised events, just as I was emotionally drawn into scenes of rioting students at the Sorbonne and of clashes between policemen and students in American universities. I was twelve, edgy and discontented, and such events gave my feelings an angry focus. I sensed upsurge and turmoil without understanding very much about it.

After Bloody Sunday in Derry, when thirteen people were shot dead by the British Army, a protest march was held in Waterford and many factory-workers left work early in order to join the demonstration. A number of people were injured when a scaffolding collapsed. In Dublin, an angry crowd set fire to the British embassy. I sat in the sitting-room listening to the radio and heard a vivid description of the burning embassy. There was a feeling — at once dangerous and attractive — of things getting out of control. Merely watching the news on television became a time of tension. No-one was allowed to talk in the kitchen. 'There was fierce trouble in the North last night,' my father would say in the morning. 'They're sending in more soldiers.'

Refugees came over the border. I had no idea what a refugee was. I imagined them as people similar to those in newsreel film from the Second World War. Then, they were always on crowded trains — the women in headscarves and heavy coats, the men carrying small bundles as they escaped across borders. The refugees who came to Waterford from the North were nothing like this. They looked just like the men and women in our street; only their accents marked them out as different. They stayed in the army barracks and one of them tried to kill himself by jumping from the top of a handball alley.

My father took me to Dublin for a day out. At lunchtime, we went to a restaurant in Mary Street, not far from the city centre and the GPO. It was a warm summer's day and the door of the restaurant was open to the street. As we sat to eat, the one o'clock news came on the radio. The volume was turned up and there was no sound except the voice of the newsreader and the busy clatter of knives and forks.

Internment had been introduced in the North the night before and scores of Catholics had been rounded up by the army and police. Women had banged dustbin lids in backyards to warn of the approaching troops. Rioting had broken out in the streets which were strewn with the wreckage of burnt-out cars and buses.

For many people, my father among them, a straight line ran from the 1916 Rising to internment and riots. His ideas on Irish politics were dominated by this line. It seemed as if the very countryside was filled with places that were emblems of what he believed in, like Geneva Barracks near Passage East where, according to a ballad, the Croppy Boy had been executed; or Vinegar Hill in County Wexford where a rebel group led by Father Murphy had battled with the British in 1798. Grey headstones and Celtic crosses stood at roadsides to mark the sites of ambush. In the weeks after Easter, the leaves on wreaths at these spots slowly wilted.

I was at dinner in my Aunt Bessie's one day when my stern grand-aunt from Carrick-on-Suir, Cáit Walsh, was paying a visit. She sent us a Christmas card which always had money in it. Otherwise, we had no contact with her. Family lore painted her as a former civil servant, my mother's aunt, who was a great one for the books. Her name was spoken with respect. This was my first time meeting her.

The subject of the North came up in the course of our dinner-time conversation. Someone mentioned Bernadette Devlin, a Catholic civil rights activist who had been elected to Westminster and had also been sentenced to jail for her role in a riot in the Bogside in Derry. 'That girl is a disgrace,' said Aunty Cáit sharply. My heart thumped quickly. Aunty Cáit sat at the table in a posture so stiff and straight that she looked as if she had a board fixed inside the back of her blouse. She held her knife as if it was a staff and said: 'The way she goes around in that mini-skirt is terrible. She has no shame.' I said nothing, for my aunt would have considered it discourteous to disagree with so eminent a member of the family. Bernadette Devlin's mini-skirt was the last thing I expected to hear mentioned. It was her fiery stance which most attracted me and, though my understanding was vague, I felt that her civil rights politics were at the heart of her importance.

I knew very little of what the North and its troubles were all about. I was approaching an age when rebels seemed more and more attractive, no matter which side they were on, and staidness, whether in personality, politics or demeanour, seemed a shin to kick against. The connection between the commemorative coin and the North was impossible for me to make. Whatever simple historical sense I possessed from family and school was becoming confused. There were rumours of men arrested in town and questioned about guns. IRA supporters marched to the Republican plot at Ballygunner cemetery. Over it all, there was a veneer of inflexibility and nostalgia with which I wanted to have nothing to do.

I put the coin away in its box, along with a medal I had won for singing, and I placed the box inside the pages of a copy of *Kidnapped* I had hollowed out with a scissors and knife. The box stayed there for years. I seldom opened it, except to look now and then at its hurt Cuchulainn and its Pearse in profile, and to wonder at the strangeness of a coin that, according to Tessie, was accumulating in value but could buy nothing.

A lamp-post stood at the end of the footpath outside the front door. Its light shone through my bedroom curtains and settled on the wall where I made silhouettes of animals with my fingers. When I looked out of the window at night, I saw moths flutter around the light. On rainy evenings, drizzle became a shower of illuminated specks.

The lamp-post, like the footpath, was one of the street's unchanging features. I would stand near it, talking to Des, for hours in the evening. Standing there, I felt the distinctive atmosphere of the seasons. The air in the street was different in autumn and spring, and an October evening in our street could have a sense of melancholic decline that was reinforced by the mist that swirled around the street-lights.

As the seasons changed and recurred, I was changing too. It was time to leave primary school after a year with Birdy Meagher. The school into which I had gone so often became a place from which I was excluded. Passing it by at the end of the street, I felt a mixture of homesickness for its classrooms and delight that I was to move on.

In sixth class, I had been in the last classroom in the school, situated at the end of an upstairs corridor near a gable wall. By leaving the school, it was as if I had somehow passed through the gable in a silent, invisible explosion and was nervously propelled towards secondary school in Mount Sion.

I now caught a bus to school every morning. After school, I often went into town and no longer came straight home. At lunchtime, I went to my aunt's house in Roanmore. In these ways, the pattern of my life changed and I started to grow away from the streets in John's Park. I sometimes arrived home in the evening at the same time as my father and this feeling of walking from town with men from factories added to my sense of change and of growing up. It also made me feel a desire to be different. I had no idea what I wanted to do but I was keen to break out of the predictable pattern.

In Mount Sion, there were more subjects to study. The spark of interest which Birdy Meagher had kindled in Latin grew and ignited. With a different teacher for every subject, it was a scene that changed every three-quarters of an hour and it had more to interest me. There was violence as well, and some lessons were no more than exercises in terror by teachers whose reputation was so strong that boys trembled when simply asked a question. Fear ran through many lessons and it could even be found in the religion class during a discussion of charity. There were teachers who never used violence and, with these, it was easier to learn. It was among this group that I found friends and inspiration.

While the world outside John's Park had been mostly confined to Dunmore East and Tramore, it now broadened to include other places. I went to the West Cork gaeltacht to learn Irish in Cúil Aodha. It was a place of which I had formed a harsh mental picture. The most famous person there was the composer Seán Ó Riada, a lean-faced man who wore striking shirts as he visited the hall where we sat at desks learning Irish. In his thirties, but grey-haired and looking much older, he spoke of the poetry and folklore of the area. A local storyteller sat on the stage telling a centuries-old story in Irish that I found impossible to understand. His hands rested on a walking-stick and he stared into space as if seeing a vision. His story poured from him with a headlong alliterative energy.

The world of the Irish language seemed tied in with the storyteller and not with the streets I knew. In school, I was in a class where almost every subject was taught through Irish. It was an unreal world, with its own shibboleths wrapped in a snobbish haze. It was also very cut off from the world in which we lived. The music to which most of the boys in my class listened was a world away from the songs we sang in the West Cork gaeltacht. Boys who during the summer had learned songs in Irish about wild goats, and lullabies to send babies to sleep, swopped Santana and Bob Dylan records once they were back in school.

I moved through the five years in Mount Sion and my world developed unsteadily. While other schools in town held discos for the pupils, Mount Sion held *céilís* which we were allowed to attend as soon as we reached fifth year. Boys sat on one side of the hall; girls on the other. A Christian Brother patrolled the floor.

I felt myself growing farther and farther away from Tessie and her world, and from the school as well. Everything was shifting from its appointed place and I was moving towards a maelstrom. Tessie was coming to the house later in the day now and her health was failing. Teacups fell from her hands and her arms sometimes shook as the first symptoms of multiple sclerosis set in. There were days when she never came to our house and eventually she stopped altogether. Her hair was turning flat and grey. Most days, I got on well with her for the short time we were together, but we had many rows as well. After these, I would feel again that confused, self-pitying longing that made me want to hide in my father's wardrobe among the old coats and cardboard shoeboxes, curled up in the darkness like a child on the run.

One August evening, I sat on a rock in Stony Cove in Dunmore East. I had the place to myself and the only noise came from waves breaking on the shore. Seaweed was strewn across the rocks along with countless pebbles. I was fifteen and just out of school after finishing fifth year. With one year to go before my Leaving Cert, I was wondering what to do when I left school.

Dunmore East had many coves and inlets, but Stony Cove was my favourite. A dirt track led down to it under a cliff near the Fisherman's Hall where my parents had met. I loved the sea at any time, but it was special on such evenings when its rhythms became my own and its calm became a quality I shared. The crowds who thronged the rocks all day had gone home. Yachts swayed in the harbour. Vague laughter carried across the water from the yacht club. A trawler headed out to sea. Quiet fell like a shawl over the evening. I watched crabs scuttle along the edges of rockpools.

I carried a book with me, as I nearly always did. It was a book of poems called *The Young British Poets* (despite the fact that it included a number of Irish poets) which I had bought out of curiosity in Waterford's single bookshop. I had read very little poetry apart from that in my schoolbooks. I read through the poems in this book with a particular intensity that I associated with such an evening in such a place. Many of the poems were beyond my understanding, but they were part of some communication that felt important. The words of the poems by themselves often seemed dull, yet as I sat reading by the sea, I found myself entering the words as if they were rooms. I was not sure whether the world narrowed to become a poem or the poems expanded to become the world. One of the poems, 'Day Trip to Donegal,' was by Derek Mahon and I read its references to the sea with such eagerness that the poem became one with the waves breaking towards me like an agent of erosion:

> *That night the slow sea washed against my head,*
> *Performing its immeasurable erosions —*
> *Spilling into the skull, marbling the stones*
> *That spine the very harbour wall,*
> *Muttering its threat to villages of landfall.*

I stopped reading when it became too dark to see the words. Suddenly, I felt very cold and headed back to my grandmother's house. I carried inside that same quietness I had known from walking through Paddy Spencer's fields, only this time it was associated with poems and with the way poets worked with words.

I tried to write my own poems. The first I wrote was a long

account of the Vietnam war, filled with vivid images of slaughter like those I saw on television. The poem ran over ten pages of a school copybook. There was a heady excitement in writing it. It came easily and without restraint, and because its lines were shaped in a certain way, I thought of it as a poem. Another poem took as its theme the sadness of people who stood by the sea.

I also wrote a love-poem. There was a girl I saw from the school-bus every morning and everything about her became an obsession. Her blonde hair was smoothly combed as she walked to school in the Ursuline Convent. She was spotlessly clean and perfectly dressed. I saw her too in the church choir and watched her go home afterwards to her house on the Ursuline Road. Words fell and flailed about when I looked for ways to describe her.

I wrote a poem for her and sent it to her. She returned it with a friend, saying she appreciated the thought but I was too young for her. I had heard of unrequited love in school and this was a startling example of the condition. I knew that it had a strong connection with poetry, so I wrote while I pined. I wrote another poem called 'Suicide'. In it, I imagined myself jumping over a cliff in Tramore and watching the sea-spray rise towards me like a million needles — an image of which I was very proud.

I sent the poem to the *Waterford News and Star* and, to my amazement, it was published there. That changed everything. I was no longer messing about. I may have been jilted, but I was a published poet.

Poetry, like the girl, became an obsession. When immersed in it as a reader or writer, my inadequacies seemed either to disappear or to find perfect expression. It was an inner life that I could make my own. I ransacked the shelves of the Waterford City Library for books of poems and read my way through the thin collections and fat anthologies. In this way, I came into contact with modern poetry which we never found in schoolbooks. Something in me connected fully with the very fact of poetry itself. It did not matter if much of it, like God and the North, was beyond my understanding.

I borrowed books by Sylvia Plath and Michael Hamburger, and also read the work of Irish poets like Thomas Kinsella, Richard Murphy and Austin Clarke, whose long poem *Mnemosyne Lay in Dust* affected me deeply, its compact verses shaping a story of chaos and breakdown. I read without plan or programme and was captivated simply by the thought of poetry. The library, with its tall brown shelves and the long tables in its reference room, became my haunt every Saturday afternoon. I took three books home in a plastic bag from the Besco supermarket, nervous of the slagging I might have to endure if seen with books of poems. I sat reading in the kitchen for hours when my father and the others had gone to bed after 'The Late Late Show'.

I looked forward to Saturday afternoon as the highlight of my week. On wet days, sitting in the reference room of the library and hearing rain beat against the high windows, it seemed that even rain had a rhythm. The shelves were stacked heavily with books. I made my way further into the world of poems, reading translations of Baudelaire, Catullus and Horace. In some way, my interest in poems was tied in with the way I viewed everything else. I had no real interest in getting a good job after school and was quickly losing interest in school itself. I felt at an angle to much of what was going on and poems were places where I found a note that immediately matched my way of looking at things.

Some of the teachers at school encouraged me. They included Jim Lusby, a temporary teacher whose attitudes seemed open and free in comparison to the stifling certainty of the Brothers who ran the school. Seán Crowe was another; he was an English teacher who was one of those in the school who could control a class without beating the pupils. In class, he suggested books that we might read: *The Tin Drum*, *The Plague*, *The Dark*, *The French Lieutenant's Woman*. Reading these books deepened my sense of freedom and exploration. In my last year at school, I read Camus' *The Outsider* and it made a sea-change within me that accelerated my sense of the oblique. Its first two sentences struck a chord that I knew intimately: 'Mother died today. Or, maybe, yesterday; I can't be sure.'

I told Seán Crowe that I was writing poems and he urged me to continue. He had encouraged other pupils over the years and some of these met at weekends in the house of a poet called Liam Murphy in Rice Park, a small housing estate not far from the school. Liam Murphy, who was in early twenties, had a reputation as a rebel. His poems appeared in many poetry magazines. He wrote in a style that eschewed punctuation and sentences, spacing his lines until they read like staccato slogans. It was a style influenced by the Liverpool poets and the rhythms of pop music. I felt uncomfortable with it but, by contending with it, I was forced to discover the rhythm of my own particular pulse. On those first Saturday afternoons it seemed part of a heady intoxication and rebellion that was suddenly running through everything and that had poetry at its core.

I joined the weekly sessions. The group was known as the Waterford Writers' Workshop. Unlike Dublin or Cork, Waterford had no literary tradition that we knew of and, as far we were concerned, our group was an idea whose time had come. We worked on simple exercises suggested by Liam Murphy: how to space lines, how to choose one word over another. These sessions gave me a sense of poetry as a craft as well as an enthusiasm and I started to spend more time at my poems, working them over until the finished piece matched the impulse that had made me write it in the first place.

Through these sessions, I also heard for the first time of writers like Basil Bunting and Douglas Dunn, whose work was to become important to me. In Douglas Dunn's book *Terry Street*, I recognised scenes that could as easily have been set outside the sitting-room window of our house in John's Park. In Basil Bunting's, I heard a music that went through me like electricity:

> *Brag, sweet tenor bull,*
> *descant on Rawthey's madrigal,*
> *each pebble its part*
> *for the fells' late spring.*
> *Dance tiptoe, bull,*
> *black against may.*
> *Ridiculous and lovely*
> *chase hurdling shadows*
> *morning into noon . . .*

Others at the workshop included Philip O'Neill, who was one class ahead of me in school, and Eddie Stapleton. Poems by them had been published in the New Irish Writing page of *The Irish Press*, a page of creative writing that I hurried to read when my father bought the paper home on Saturdays and to which I sent dozens of poems that all came back with rejection slips. Liam Murphy's poems had been published in a small book by Tara Telephone Publications, a publishing house that later became The Gallery Press, and this lent him credibility and importance.

One of his poems was also published in a special magazine issued by the school to mark the anniversary of the Sodality of Mary Immaculate. It read like a poem in praise of a Christian Brother who had once taught in the school. The magazine was distributed (copies even went to Rome, we were told). I wondered at what seemed Murphy's charitable and generous attitude towards this man of whom he, like myself and many others, spoke disparagingly. The word then went around that the poem was an acrostic, and that on reading the initial letter of each line, one discovered a sentence which said that the Brother in question, who had been praised in every line, *was a fucker.*

I had known nothing of this acrostic. Liam Murphy had deliberately not told me because he knew it could cause trouble for me in school. I was called aside and questioned about it nonetheless. One of the Brothers called me into the science room, where black taps were curved on benches and the air had a heavy chemical smell.

'This man, Murphy. How often do you see him?'

'Every Saturday.'

'And what sort of a relationship do you have with him?' His question was embarrassing and ridiculous and I did not answer it.

'Well, what do you talk about when you all meet in his house?'

'Poems.'

'Are you still going to Mass?'

'No.'

Awkwardness and hurt mixed in his face. 'I'll pray for you so,' he said. 'You can go.'

Hundreds of copies of the magazine were taken back. The poem was excised and replaced with a poem in Irish about the 1916 Rising.

This was not the only time poetry brought me under suspicion in the school. Seán Crowe suggested that I and some others in the class should organise poetry and music sessions in the school library on Friday evenings. At the first such session, I read from some new books of poems that Seán Crowe had loaned me, including *Orchestra of Silence* by Gerard Smyth. I liked the book and read some poems from it. Others played songs by Leonard Cohen and Bob Dylan, and the evening was generally thought to be a success, though the Brothers appeared suspicious of it.

I was walking through a corridor on my way out of the school when one of the Brothers (who had not been at the session) stopped me. He held me by the arm. Chalk-dust flecked his clothes.

'Well, how did it go? The session.'

'It went fine.' I was nervous.

He looked straight past me as he spoke. 'Ye were reading poems. Was this one of the books?' He took the book of poems from my hand and leafed through it, glancing quizzically at each page. 'This is not the kind of poetry we had when we were in school.' He stopped at a page and read for what seemed like minutes. All the time, he kept his hand tightly on my arm. I was as tall as him, but he never looked me in the eye.

'Did you read this poem tonight?' he asked. It was a poem called 'Slowdance.'

'Yes,' I told him. His grip on my arm tightened. My classmates passed in the corridor and slowed down to stare. My heart hurried.

'And did you read these lines?' He let my arm go and pointed at the last verse:

> *Sensitive,*
> *Yet sensual, is the young girl waiting*
> *In a blouse she wears for his hot hands,*
> *When the slowdance ends,*
> *And they hide in a bush of stars.*

'Yes,' I said. My monosyllabic answer made it sound like a courtroom inquisition. And like a barrister who has trapped a witness, he began his final assault. In the same way as I had seen a Christian Brother act with Jimmy O'Leary in the primary school years before, he caught me by the ear and pulled me towards him. I could smell cigarettes on his breath. Then he caught me by the hair just next to my ear, pulling and pushing me as he spoke.

'What do you think of that poem, as you call it?' he asked. My high ideals became a whirlwind in my head.

'I think it's art,' I said. This sounded like the height of cheekiness.

'Art?' he echoed. He spoke the word as if it turned his stomach. 'That's not art'. He tugged at my hair and pulled me closer. 'That,' he said firmly, 'is *filth*. Do you hear me? *Filth*.'

He let me go. My ear was stinging and I was a mass of confusion. I was angry and humiliated as he walked away, and I felt as well that the world he represented was one with which I would have nothing to do.

Poetry continued to attract me and became even more important when I realised that it had a certain subversive standing. I had another experience similar to my evening in Stony Cove, only this time it took place near a bridge to which I had cycled. The bridge was a few miles from John's Park and I sat in the field behind it with a heavy copy of Wordsworth's *Prelude*. I knew some of Wordsworth's poetry from school and especially liked his poem 'Tintern Abbey'. I sometimes found in his work what seemed an expression of the way I felt about poetry and about the world. I got this same sense in the early sections of *The Prelude*. I started to read it and stayed reading for hours, my back resting against the warm stones of the bridge underneath which a thin stream dripped over stones. The poem drew me in:

> *Fair seed-time had my soul, and I grew up*
> *Fostered alike by beauty and by fear:*
> *Much favoured in my birthplace, and no less*
> *In that beloved Vale to which ere long*

> *We were transplanted — there were we let loose*
> *For sports of wider range.*

I had often been drawn into the world of novels, caught up by a story and held by the suspense and excitement of a plot. The effect of poetry was different. I was carried along in the same way, but it was the thrill of recognition rather than of plot. It was as if everything that had ever happened to me and made me the kind of person I was had now fused in poetry and its power. It was as if I had become airborne and earthed at once. By trying to write, I had found a way to be myself.

As had happened in the cove, I stopped reading when darkness fell. I looked around at the fields. Cattle stood in the grass. Trees in the distance seemed Wordsworthian, infused with the poem and echoing what the poet called 'the ghostly language of the ancient earth'.

I got on my bike and cycled home, moving at an easy pace past houses, ditches, and gates that were run through with the spirit of what I had read. It felt as if a world that was usually separate and alternative to my everyday world had now joined with it. When I got home, I wanted to write, but was unable: the language seemed an empty echo of *The Prelude* and it was days before I felt that words could be my own again.

The streets seemed narrower by the day. Gardens that years before had looked as large as playgrounds now seemed just plain suburban gardens. The adults around me were growing older and childhood was a skin I was starting to shed. The fields stretching towards Paddy Spencer's farm became predictable paths that I grew tired of exploring. In Dunmore

East, too many people knew me through my family. In John's Park, the same men came home from work every evening; the same women stood talking at the doorsteps or outside the shop.

'Have you made up your mind what you're going to be?' my Aunt Bessie asked me. I did not want to be anything. In school we heard about different jobs, but none of them interested me. I sat exams for positions in the civil service. I filled in forms for jobs in banks and insurance offices. I sensed that a job defined a person in some finished way, and because I felt undefined, I had no desire to get one. The only thing I really seemed to feel was the pressure of change and questioning. Whatever was to happen, it would be tied in with writing.

John's Park became smaller and smaller, and Waterford seemed to shrink too. No matter where I went, the scene had a deadening familiarity about it. There was a sense of constriction about the shops I passed in Ballybricken or in Broad Street, or about the gates of the Erin's Own Hurling and Football Club that I passed each day in Poleberry.

I walked along the quays and leaned against the chains that acted as railings between the quayside and the river Suir. I heard a train pull into the railway station on the other side and saw cars heading towards Ferrybank. The river broke gently against the quayside. Looking to my right, I could see the shops stretching down the quays on the other side of the road. I knew their names from childhood: Hearnes, where I remembered change and receipts whirring from one assistant to another along wires above the counters; Shaws, where one of my cousins worked in the shoe department; Chapmans, with its smells of coffee, cheese and spices, and its name written in a mosaic on the ground at the entrance; the Granville Hotel, where my mother, smiling, had once posed for a photograph.

I longed for somewhere free of such associations. There

were shops right down the quays, past the Clock Tower and on towards Reginald's Tower, around towards the Mall and the Tower Hotel near the small Atlas Library where I had gone first with my grandmother.

Looking to my left, I could see more shops on the footpaths behind me, but I could also see the bridge. It was called Redmond bridge after John Redmond. The bridge formed one way out of Waterford. It led to the Dublin and Kilkenny road. The road to Cork was on the other side of the city.

A man wheeled a bicycle across the bridge with a suitcase tied to the bar. I saw the sky redden behind him, framed by the steel interstices of the bridge. It was a sky like a scene from a Renaissance painting of the Creation. The clouds were pierced by light. Red and orange mingled as the day died. The sky seemed more vast and clear than I had ever seen it.

One of the roads underneath that sky led to the paper mills where my father worked. Another led to the foundry. A third led to the Clover Meats factory. Smoke from a factory chimney rose into the sky and the water on the river trembled. Pylons studded the hills on either side of the Suir. Only the river and the sky excited me. The city was a background with which I had become too familiar while the sky was a vast unknown. I saw it with a hugeness that was impossible in John's Park where the roofs framed the clouds. A train whistle sounded in the railway station where one of my uncles worked. The train pulled out, gathering speed as it went past the river on the way to Rosslare, the rhythmic movement of its wheels gathering force as it sped.

It was time for me to get out as well.